malibu NANNY

ADVENTURES OF THE FORMER
KARDASHIAN NANNY

PAM BEHAN

WITH SARA CHRISTENSON

MN PRESS

MINNESOTAGIRLS

MALIBU NANNY:
ADVENTURES OF THE FORMER KARDASHIAN NANNY

For information, contact Minnesota Girls Press at info@MinnesotaGirlsPress.com.

Cover and graphic elements: Sabrina Hale in association with Hoopla Worldwide, LLC

Book design: Janet Hirata Stall

ISBN 978-0-9890331-0-7 (ebook)
ISBN 978-0-9890331-1-4 (print)

For My Son, Jamie

Author's Note
Some names have been changed to protect identities.

INTRODUCTION

This book is about my journey. A rite of passage that started in a small town in the Midwest. Growing up, I dreamed of great adventure and excitement. I hoped to travel the world and accomplish noble things. As happens in life, it didn't quite turn out the way I planned. Following my best friend to California after graduating from high school, I ended up working as a nanny for nearly a decade for two families who were successful and somewhat famous in their own right at the time. Imagine my surprise fifteen years later when those two families — the Jenners and Kardashians — became one of the most famous blended families in the world.

That decade in Hollywood taught me a great deal about life, helped to define my priorities, and prepared me for motherhood. During the five years I worked for her, Kris Jenner taught me how to be tenacious at multitasking; and my eight years working for Bruce Jenner instilled inspirational qualities that have impacted my life personally and professionally.

I was just a kid myself when I started working as a nanny, and I made some big mistakes along the way. Yet, each twist, turn, and stumble along my path led me to where I am now. Character is developed and wisdom is gained only through trial and error. It's the times we fall down and get really hurt that lead to our greatest triumphs. My proudest accomplishment is being a good mother to my young son, and I see how every step on my path contributed and led to this blessing.

My journey was also a discovery of spirituality. The awkward, fear-based religious experience of my youth transitioned to many years when I didn't give God much thought. Desperate and lonely amidst deep hurt and disappointment, I finally turned back to God, discovering a new relationship with Him, defined by love, grace, and forgiveness.

I always kept on dreaming and taking chances, yet stayed true to who I was. Even when things didn't turn out as I planned, and I made bad mistakes, I continually held on to hope. I chose to believe in my dreams and tried to learn from my poor decisions.

When I maintain the right attitude, yet stay authentic, *every* day of my life can be an adventure.

But I'm getting ahead of myself.

It was the spring of my senior year of high school in Norcross, Minnesota (population 123), one thousand eight hundred and fifty miles away from Los Angeles (population 8,419,000). My grand adventure was about to begin…

CHAPTER ONE
Big Dreams

I nervously tug on my turtleneck sweater as I walk to the front of Mrs. Itzen's College Prep English class. Looking down at my notes, I notice for the first time that my mom polished my favorite white and red leather Nikes. Probably because she knew I had a speech today, I reason. I turn around, and fifteen smiling faces greet me expectantly. Mrs. Itzen nods her head.

"Okay, Pam. Go ahead."

Clearing my throat, I begin. "My speech today is called 'Why I Want to Be a Cruise Director,' by Pam Behan."

It is the spring of 1987, and as my high school graduation quickly approaches, I hold big dreams for my future. One of my favorite television shows is *The Love Boat*, and the cruise director, Julie, embodies all I want to be. She is fun loving, energetic, cute, bubbly, and lives a glamorous life, sailing to exotic locations around the globe. Each week, another crazy adventure entangles Julie and the crew, always involving the eccentric, famous and sometimes outright nutty passengers. I am hooked. That's how I want my life to be. She always seems so happy. It is enticing. And, it could combine my two loves of sports and music. If I was the cruise director, I conclude, I could lead aerobics and referee basketball games during the day, and entertain my guests at the piano in an elegant ball gown at night.

"I want to be a cruise director for three main reasons," I state enthusiastically, following Mrs. Itzen's rule to always develop three or five main points, and then introduce them at the beginning of a speech.

"Number one, I will get to travel around the world to many interesting and exciting destinations. Number two, I will enjoy directing activities for the

1

passengers and ensuring that they have fun. And, number three, I will meet many amazing new people."

I look up, as Mrs. Itzen had taught me, to connect with my audience. She is nodding her head again, and with the exception of one smirk, everyone else is smiling, so I take a deep breath, and finish my speech with confidence.

I want to explore the world beyond the confines of the small town I now call home. I hope to experience the thrill of great adventure, taste a bit of danger, and conquer new challenges. Setting sail around the world on a cruise ship seems to be a good avenue to achieve my dreams.

With a population of just over a hundred, Norcross, Minnesota, requires only one main intersection with a four-way stop. It also boasts a small grocery store, a café, and a couple of churches, and that's about it. If you blink on the highway that runs through town, you might miss it.

Growing up in a small town feels like warm apple pie, a favorite soft blanket, and a steaming cup of hot chocolate with whipped cream on a cold day. Comfort, pure and simple. It's also kind of like having a big extended family who all live within a few blocks of you. There are a few "crazy aunts" and "kooky uncles," but for the most part, they're all genuine, down to earth, good people. The funny thing (or not so funny depending on how you look at it) about a small town is how everybody knows your business. They learn your routine, what time you leave in the morning, what time you get home, and what you do every day, and when that routine is disrupted, folks know about it. If you're sick and in bed and turn the lights out much earlier than usual, you might get a phone call or knock on the door asking if you're okay. That's just how it is in a small town.

After school, I'd run out the door, yelling a hasty, "Bye Mom," and head down the street to play football or baseball with my friends. As evening approached, Mom would yell loudly from our front door several blocks away, "Time for supper," and I'd skip back home. There were no strangers, only neighbors and friends. When a new car drives through town, necks crane to figure out, who is the intruder? Several days a week, especially on weekends, friends drop by unannounced for a cup of coffee and a chat.

MALIBU NANNY

The Norcross Café a few blocks from my house is a warm and reliable beacon of light in early morning, as farmers dressed in overalls and baseball caps drive in to town as early as five a.m., to pour themselves a cup of coffee at the tiny, quaint restaurant, settle on a stool at the counter, and chat with each other about the weather, the crops, and the gossip around town.

My mom is "Suzy Homemaker." She makes the most scrumptious lemon bars, wears bright cotton candy pink lipstick, and loves interior design. Our house — a small, single-level, three-bedroom home that looks like a page torn from *Better Homes and Gardens* — is *always* filled with delicious aromas. My brother and I often return home from school, lessons, or practice to the smell of something freshly baked. Besides her famous lemon bars, mint brownies, seven-layer bars, chocolate chip cookies, peanut butter cookies, and pies are some of her other specialties. When she makes pie, she always makes two — cherry for me (I don't like blueberry), and blueberry for my brother (he doesn't like cherry). Mom aims to please.

My dad was born in a house in Norcross and lived there for most of his life. When he graduated from high school, he joined the Army and was stationed in Germany for a while. In his early twenties, after being discharged, Dad began his lifelong career as an insurance salesman. However, his true love is nature — hunting, fishing, boating, camping, and hiking. Consequently, much of my childhood has been filled with outdoor activities.

Splitting, drying, stacking, and moving wood is a big task that we have to accomplish every year. We have a wood-burning stove that heats the whole house during the long Minnesota winter, and boy, does it get cold. When it's thirty degrees below zero and the wind is blowing seventy-five miles per hour, you get frostbite in a matter of minutes. It doesn't matter how many layers of clothing you put on; you just can't stay warm. To keep our house heated during the very cold winter, we cut and stack endless mounds of wood. As a matter of fact, it seems like all we do during the summer is gather wood for the winter months.

Occasionally, I (along with a group of Norcross kids) am hired by a local farmer to "pick rocks" — clearing all the bigger rocks out of their field so that it will be smooth, and easier to plow and plant. Not an easy job, but some of the most fun I can remember. I am always the only girl in our group of rock pickers. We laugh, joke, run around, and look forward to snack time and lunchtime, which is always a feast. Most farmers' wives put out quite a spread.

Because I live in a small town, there aren't too many kids, and most of them are boys. The only girl in town close to my age is Tanya, and she doesn't even actually live here. Her grandma has a house in Norcross, and Tanya visits often from Minneapolis, so I love spending time with her when she's around.

So as a young girl, I'd often end up playing with the guys. We started calling ourselves "The Norcross Gang" — brothers Nathan and Clayton, Brent aka "Bubba" (who cried once when I beat him in football) and his brother Curt, my brother, and me. We spent a lot of time playing baseball and football, and I earned the nickname "Crusher" for my speed and running skills. In the sixth grade, I actually won the Punt, Pass and Kick contest, beating all of the boys in my class.

Because of my guy friends and my outdoor activities, I gained a reputation as a tomboy — a small town girl who gathers wood, picks rock, can shoot a gun, hunt, fish, play baseball and football, and run like nobody's business.

On the very first day of Kindergarten, I met Sara, and by the end of the day, we were best friends. Many of my weekends were spent at Sara's farm in the country. We made up cheer and dance routines on the big green lawn, fixed each other's hair and makeup, and baked cookies. We told ghost stories before bed, dressed up in costumes and put on plays, built play houses in the trees, and made forts in the snow. We were two peas in a pod, best friends, and soul mates — the sister each of us never had. At school, when a teacher would see me by myself, she would ask, "Where is Sara?" They often got our names mixed up.

Our favorite activity was sitting at the piano together, singing silly songs like "Peter Peter Pumpkin Eater." Hours and hours were spent at that piano together, laughing, playing and singing. It was Sara that inspired my love of piano. I begged my parents to let me take lessons. They finally gave in but with a caveat. I had to prove to them that I wasn't going to quit before they would buy me a piano. Every day for a year — snow, rain, or bitter cold — I walked about a half mile to our church to practice piano. Now that's commitment. At the end of the year, my parents bought me a beautiful Wurlitzer piano.

Piano and music became a huge part of my life. I continued taking lessons and played piano throughout elementary and high school. I also became the accompanist for the choirs at school.

I always loved music. When I was about eight, I got a record player and an Elvis record for Christmas. The record had "All Shook Up" on one side and "Shake, Rattle & Roll" on the other side. I played that record over and over, singing and dancing to the songs. As the records spun, the notes of the music wrapped around my heart, and I fell in love with Elvis.

A year later, as I was watching *The Wizard of Oz* at my Grandma's house one day, the program was interrupted by a news bulletin — Elvis had died. I started crying and screaming. I was devastated. My grandma ran into the living room, thinking I was injured. She was quite surprised to find I was wailing over Elvis.

As much as I was drawn to music, the tomboy side of me was pulled towards athletics. Because the high school we went to in nearby Herman (another small town of only six hundred people) had less than a hundred students, extracurricular activities weren't ultra competitive. (The only team that had tryouts was cheerleading.) I was able to be involved in pretty much any activity I chose. My sports were basketball, volleyball, football cheerleading, and track.

Throughout my high school years, music and sports have been my passions. Schoolwork on the other had is *not* a passion. It is only something

that gets in the way of my extracurricular activities. Class clown, social butterfly, goofball, and joker — all these terms apply to me. At the beginning of senior year, I was voted Rowdiest, Class Clown, Most Athletic, Most Musical, Most Talkative, Most Gullible, and Best Sense of Humor. They definitely sum me up. I find humor in any situation, and I'm always looking for an opportunity to crack a joke. I'm usually singing, dancing, laughing, joking and smiling. Even in stressful or difficult situations, I often find a way to lighten the mood or crack a joke to make someone smile. I've never had a problem with making a fool of myself to hear the sweet sound of laughter.

Because I love to goof around and have fun, I thought babysitting might be a good fit for me — a chance to be silly with young kids. So in junior high I started taking care of my neighbor kids, Nicholas and Katie. They became a huge part of my life, as I babysat for them often. Always the jokester, I got an empty chewing tobacco tin from my Grandpa one day and filled it with chocolate cake crumbs. The next time I babysat Nicholas, I took the tin out of my pocket and shook it. Then I took a "dip" of chocolate cake crumbs and pretended to choke on it. He stared at me, wide-eyed and shocked. I quickly showed him I was only teasing, and a huge grin covered his face. I was pretty sure he'd never take up chewing tobacco. I *loved* those kids. I realized I had a real knack for babysitting. I was a big kid myself, and loved to play games, laugh, joke and have fun. It was a perfect fit. Being responsible and caring for the children is an important part of the deal of course, but if kids don't like you, you probably won't be asked back. And kids *always* love me.

My family goes to a local church every Sunday — Our Savior's Lutheran Church. That's what you do in a small town in the Midwest. One doesn't question it. You listen to your teacher at school Monday through Friday, see the dentist every six months and brush your teeth like a good girl, make your bed every morning because your mom says so, and do what the pastor says to do. That pretty much sums up my experience of God, religion, and church.

I *guess* I love God…because that's what I am supposed to do, but I don't really know Him. And I'm quite certain He doesn't know me. I'm pretty sure He has a lot more important things to worry about.

I've been the organist of my church since sixth grade. Every Sunday morning, I take my place at the organ in front of the church. The boys I hang out with attend the church as well. They sit in the back row together and make faces at me. It makes me smile, and sometimes I have to cough or cover my mouth to keep from laughing. When I glance at my mom, her stern face of disapproval sobers me up pretty quick.

That's a good analogy of how I feel about God and my religious experience. My carefree spirit wants to have fun and be happy (yet of course be good in the eyes of God), but I always feel like I can't quite get it right. I try really, really hard to be that good girl, and not make God mad at me, but, fear of God pretty much defines my relationship with Him.

Despite the guilt of trying to live up to the list of rules I feel God operates with, overall I'm a fairly happy teenager. With graduation coming up soon, I'm excited and anxious to explore the world beyond this isolated sphere.

I am thoroughly committed to pursuing my career goal of being a cruise director. When I started looking for colleges a few months ago, however, I was surprised to find out that there were not many schools that offer travel courses or majors. I found one small college that offers a Travel/Tourism Major called National American University in Rapid City, SD. I was still unsure, so I tried out for the volleyball team, and made it, which sealed the deal for me.

So here I am, a few months before I graduate, and my future lies before me — a blank canvas. I have such high hopes for my life. I can't wait to get out of this small town where I've grown up. Not that there's anything particularly bad about it, it's just that I've matured beyond what this place can offer me. I want more. I want adventure, discovery, and new experiences. I hope to see the world.

But do I have what it takes? I hope I can handle a full-time college schedule while playing on a college volleyball team. What will my roommates be like? Will I find a job when I graduate? Will a cruise ship hire me? And what if Mr. Right shows up? A serious relationship would only delay or prevent me from achieving my goals, so I am committed to steering clear of suitors. Yet, I'm wise enough to know sometimes the most carefully constructed plans can be interrupted when love hits you upside the head. I hope that doesn't happen. I imagine myself knee deep in diapers and screaming toddlers, travelling only in my daydreams, and shudder at the thought. Someday, but not anytime soon.

Graduation is a flurry of excitement, and after the longest summer of my life, fall finally arrives. My parents drive me to Rapid City, and drop me at my new dormitory. I'm filled with expectation and excitement at what awaits me. I harbor so many hopes and dreams in my heart, with blind and pure belief that I *can* and *will* make them become my reality.

Being away from home, making my own decisions, living with fun roommates, and playing on the volleyball team — who knew life on your own without parental supervision could be so fun and carefree? I move into co-ed dorms with three roommates — Kelley, Marci, and Tracy. Kelley and Marci are also on the volleyball team, so as "athletes" we are quite popular. We attend parties, host parties, crash parties, and plan our weeks around parties. Schoolwork is more of an after thought than a main priority.

I get my first "real" job at ARBY'S fast food restaurant, and meet Billie Jo, who becomes my closest friend in Rapid City. We usually work the same shift, and often borrow her sister's dilapidated old car that barely runs, and drive up to Mt. Rushmore, listening to music on the car radio, talking about life, and laughing. Being away from home and living a life of complete independence is great fun and an adventure in itself. But, I long for more.

College graduation seems like a lifetime away. I am chomping at the bit to fulfill my quest to explore life beyond the Midwest.

Despite my new friends and college life, I miss my best friend, Sara, who is now attending the University of Southern California in Los Angeles. The draw of Hollywood and the Southern California experience are very appealing to me. In addition to *The Love Boat,* two of my other favorite TV shows growing up were *CHiPS* and *Charlie's Angels,* both set in Los Angeles. These shows were filled with fast cars, lots of action, beaches, warm weather, sexy people, sexy clothes, and the glitz and glamour of Hollywood. I was infatuated with Erik Estrada, and obsessed with the three Angels: Farrah Fawcett, Jaclyn Smith, and Cheryl Ladd. I identified with them and yearned to be like them. They were glamorous, gorgeous women who carried guns and drove fast cars. Because of my tomboy background, their combination of femininity and toughness really appealed to me.

So, after my first year of college, I decide to get a nanny job in California just for the summer. My thirst for adventure can't wait until I graduate from college, and I don't want to go back to Norcross. Sara doesn't yet know where she'll be staying that summer, so I can't count on  rooming with her. Being a live-in nanny seems like a perfect fit. I babysat Nicholas and Katie for four years, so I figure I am well qualified to be a nanny. I have also heard that young girls from the Midwest are much sought after. I will have room and board provided, and I will be able to save up some money as well.

It is all going to work out perfectly. I will return the next fall to continue classes in Rapid City. But in the meantime, a summer of fun and excitement in Hollywood — the glamorous land of movie and TV stars — awaits me.

CHAPTER TWO
Hollywood, Here I Come

As the plane descends over Los Angeles towards the airport, I look down in disbelief. I am amazed the city is so enormous and never-ending. Row after row of houses spread out below me like lines of dominoes. For a nineteen year old, small town girl from Minnesota, it is quite an adventure to be in such a huge city.

My stomach churns with the anticipation of seeing Hollywood, and the glamour and wealth I am sure to encounter. I look forward to a fun, exciting summer with my best friend in the big city. I certainly hope to meet some celebrities, but I'm not expecting it. I envision a grand adventure, and hope to spend a lot of time soaking up the sun and enjoying the amazing weather at the beach. A summer romance wouldn't be too awful either.

Sara picks me up at the airport. Giddy with excitement at seeing each other after nearly a year apart, we can't stop talking. On our way to Sara's apartment in Pasadena, where she is staying for the summer so she can be close to her boyfriend who lives there, she turns onto a side street, as we chat excitedly about our summer plans. Wham! A car rams into the back left tire area. We realize quickly Sara turned the wrong way down a one-way street. I've been in Los Angeles for only a few hours, and I've already been in a car accident. This is not a good omen.

The other driver calls the police, and we fill out a police report. After exchanging insurance information and checking the damage, we head to Sara's apartment. According to our not-so-expert analysis, the damage appears minor.

The next day we have plans to go to the beach, and since the car seems to drive okay, Sara decides to wait to get it checked out. The sun, sand, and surf are calling our names.

We drive to a beach in Santa Monica, which is about forty-five minutes from Sara's apartment. The view leaves me breathless — blue cloudless sky, endless white sand, blue water, palm trees, and the smell of coconut oil in the air from the many bronzed sun worshippers lining the beach. This is going to be a great summer, I think.

We enjoy a lovely day of lounging on our towels in the sun. We buy hot dogs and lemonade at a stand on the beach, and later indulge in ice cream cones. As the sun kisses the afternoon goodbye, with our skin pink and our spirits relaxed and happy, we head home.

On the Pasadena Freeway, halfway to Sara's apartment, the back left wheel falls off her car. We watch the tire take off in front of us, rolling down the road, while our left axel screeches along the concrete, sparks shooting everywhere, until the car comes to a stop at the side of the road. Jumping out, we stand at the edge of the freeway staring at the car, clueless about what to do next.

I start laughing hysterically, because I'm nervous and don't know what else to do. Sara glares at me.

"How can you be laughing at a time like this?"

It makes me laugh even harder.

We are so relieved when a good samaritan stops to help. He pulls up behind us, gets out of his car, and screams, "Well, are you going to put the fire out?"

We are standing next to the car, but on the opposite side of the damaged wheel, and we didn't realize the axle was on fire. The man bends down and scoops up dirt onto the fire. Without another word, he drives off, disgustedly shaking his head. He must think we are pretty dumb. Not dumb. Just young, naive, small town girls from Minnesota, Sir.

We call a tow truck. The driver hitches up the car, and gives us a lift back to Sara's apartment in Pasadena.

The next day, I call a nanny agency in Beverly Hills. They are extremely interested in meeting me, confirming what I had heard about Midwest girls being in high demand, and set up an appointment with me for the following day.

Since Sara's car is indisposed due to our unfortunate accident, she has to take the bus to her summer job. As I have no other options for transportation, I also have to jump on a bus to make it to my interview. The trip from Pasadena to Beverly Hills takes a *very* long time. I get to see some lovely parts of the inner city, and meet some rather interesting people on the bus ride. I am friendly, outgoing, and talk to everyone, believing in the adage, "There are no strangers, only friends I've yet to meet."

As I step off the bus in the heart of Beverly Hills, I gaze in absolute awe at my surroundings. Rolls Royce, Mercedes, Jaguar, Porsche, and Ferrari are some of the exotic cars I see lining the streets. I was so anxious to get out of Norcross, and now here I am amidst the glamour of Beverly Hills. I am impressed and overwhelmed by the people, the cars, the buildings, and the fashions. I feel as if I have been dropped right into a movie. I buy into the lifestyle right then and there. I want to be a part of this, I tell myself.

Everywhere I look are men in fancy business suits, and glamorous women with perfect hair and designer handbags. I feel completely out of place. When I dressed for my interview this morning, I thought I looked pretty good. Now, I examine my outfit, which screams, "not from here." I am wearing a white shirt dress from Avon that hits me about mid-calf and a thin white belt around my waist. My frizzy, permed hair is pinned up in front and hanging loose in back. My bangs are hot ironed into one perfect, smooth curl.

From head to toe, I fear it is glaringly obvious that I do not fit in — not in Southern California and certainly not in Beverly Hills. As I walk into the professional office building where the nanny agency is located, I am feeling completely self-conscious. But then I think, maybe my awkward, straight from the country look might actually benefit me, since it will be obvious that they have the 100%, genuine, real-deal, Midwestern girl on their hands, who will undoubtedly make a great motherly nanny, because what else could she possibly do in this town dressed like that? So I decide not to let it bother me. I sling my denim purse with an "I Love Elvis" pin over my shoulder, fluff up my frizzy curly bangs a little bit more, lift my chin, put a smile on my face, and march proudly into the office.

The receptionist greets me, and I am ushered into the office of my assigned agent, Mr. Jacobson. I look around the room, surveying the beautiful, obviously expensive furniture. Exquisite works of art cover the walls, and a huge vase of fresh flowers sits on a table in the corner. The office window offers a stunning view, overlooking all of Beverly Hills. What a contrast to the small town life I've come from. The only office I'd spent much time in back home was my dad's home office that he used for his insurance business. The wood paneled walls were adorned with two prized fish my dad and I caught, and wildlife prints by renowned South Dakota artist, Terry Redlin. On the sturdy, big desk sat a mounted pheasant Dad shot. As a little girl, I loved to crawl into his lap as he sat in his comfortable leather chair that squeaked pleasantly. I remember the sweet, pungent smell of his ever-present tobacco pipe. I felt comfortable there. Here I feel like an outsider in a world I know nothing about.

I fill out an application as instructed, and nervously wait for Mr. Jacobson to arrive, wondering about the family that would choose me. Will the kids be really young or school age? Will they like me? Will they treat me like family or keep a professional distance? Excitement mingles with fear of the unknown.

Mr. Jacobson finally enters the room. He is a tall, slender man dressed elegantly in a three-piece suit. His hair is cut very short, and he is clean-shaven, with small wire-rimmed glasses poised at the end of his long slender nose. He is polite, but somewhat reserved. He sits down in the chair behind his desk, pulls out a notebook, and peers at me over his glasses.

"So, Ms. Behan, tell me about your experience with children," Mr. Jacobson asks.

"Well, I babysat my neighbor kids, Nicholas and Katie, for four years."

"Okay. That's fine," he responds. "And what were your duties as a babysitter for them?"

"I played with them, put them to bed, fed them. You know. All the stuff babysitters do," I offer in explanation. I am not quite sure what he wants to hear.

"That's fine, Pam. Did you cook meals for them?"

"Well, not exactly. I mean Cindy usually had something for me to heat up for them in the microwave."

I hope that my lack of experience with cooking won't be a strike against me. I don't know how to cook or bake. My mom always did all of the cooking, and the kitchen was her domain, and hers alone. She never really taught me much about cooking or baking.

"Okay, that's fine," he says again.

But I am beginning to realize it is not fine. He doesn't like my answers. I shift in my seat and begin to twist a piece of my hair between my fingers.

He continues, "And did you drive the kids to their activities or play dates or anything like that?"

"Umm. Well, no. I lived right next door to them, so I didn't have to drive, and they were really little. If they wanted a play date, we would just walk to a friend's house."

I am concerned now. I don't seem to be answering the questions the way he expects me to.

"Oh, I see. Well didn't you drive them to t-ball practice or ballet classes or violin lessons or something like that?" he asks sincerely.

I couldn't suppress my smile. I grin widely.

"Mr. Jacobson, where I come from, we don't really have stuff like that. I pretty much just played with the kids."

He doesn't return my smile. Mr. Jacobson continues to question me about my background, my year of college, and why I want to work as a nanny in Los Angeles.

It is hard to tell how things are going, because this guy doesn't crack a smile or give me any indication that he likes me at all. Since I haven't been asked to leave yet, I assume it is going okay.

Mr. Jacobson says he has one final question.

"Do you want to be a live-in nanny or a live-out nanny?"

"Hmmm. Let me think about that for a second. Well I don't have any money and I have no place to live, soooo….how 'bout live-in?"

I think it's funny, but he just looks at me without any hint of a smile.

"Okay, we're all set. I should have a few interviews lined up for you in the next couple of days. I will give you a call."

After my interview, I walk down Rodeo Drive, smiling as I think of one of my friends from the "country" back home who calls it "Roh-Dee-Oh" Drive. I pass Fendi, Gucci, and Chanel, peeking through the windows into the pristine shops with perfectly shined floors, where a handful of wealthy patrons peruse the racks of glimmering and glittering merchandise. I dare not venture inside, dressed as I am, for fear that I will be escorted right back outside, since it is fairly obvious that I can't afford to buy even the cheapest item from any one of the stores. I doubt I can even afford one shoelace.

What a contrast to the downtown area of Norcross. The one-block hub of the town consists of a small grocery store, the café, a tiny gas station with two pumps, a welding shop, a post office, and a town hall. The town hall is a gathering place where folks vote, and children sit on Santa Claus's lap at Christmas. There is another hall a few blocks away near our church. Its claim to fame, which everyone in town brags about, was a performance in the 1940's by Lawrence Welk, who hosted a variety show called *The Lawrence Welk Show* on TV for three decades. The same stage that had once been graced by Mr. Welk also hosted local theater productions in the decades before I was born.

The hall has been closed to the public for many years, but the kids in The Norcross Gang played basketball there often. Although the front doors were locked, a side door was always open, and we'd sneak inside and play on the creaky, dusty wood floor. We could only play during the day, because there was no electricity — the large windows, covered in layers of dirt and grime, filtered hazy light onto the floor, illuminating the billows of dust as we ran around.

My thoughts of home dissipate, as I spot my first "star"— Angie Dickinson from a TV show called *Police Woman*. I hold my breath and stare at her. It was my brother's favorite show and since we had only one television, I ended up watching it too. I can't believe it. I had hoped to meet many stars this summer, but I wasn't really expecting it to happen, and certainly not this soon. After watching Angie for years from my tiny living room thousands of miles away, to actually see her in person is surreal. I feel as though I know her. I want to get her autograph. Imagine what my brother will think. But fear stops me. Besides, I really just want to watch her for a while.

So, instead, I follow her as she shops, ducking behind a rack of clothes or into a doorway when she turns, to make sure she doesn't catch me following her. She looks beautiful and glamorous, wearing a big floppy white hat and dark sunglasses. Who am I going to see next? After an hour of searching for more celebrities on Rodeo Drive with no luck, I give up and jump on the bus for the long ride back to Pasadena.

I don't know when a nanny job will open up, so I decide to make my rounds at the mall in Pasadena near Sara's apartment to get a job. I land a position as a sales associate at JCPenney, and start work immediately. It's a good distraction — something to do while Sara is at work all day — and I definitely need the money.

Mr. Jacobson contacts me a few days later. He has an interview lined up for me that week with Linda Jenner in Malibu. My mind starts to spin with visions of palm trees, palatial beach homes, white sand beaches, and gorgeous, muscular, tanned surfers parading up and down the sand.

On the day of my appointment with Linda, I ride the bus from Pasadena to Malibu. I pour over the bus route maps, hoping I will actually end up at my intended destination. The bus route is a long, roundabout way to Malibu — a trip that takes nearly two hours. We meander through an area called "The Valley," seemingly going in circles, onto a winding road named

Malibu Canyon that cuts through the mountain range to the beach and offers breathtaking views of the canyon.

During the bus ride, I jot down a list of rules for being a good nanny. Maybe I'll go over it with Linda during the interview.

Rules for Being a Good Nanny

1. Love the children unconditionally, as if they were my own.
2. Discipline the kids consistently and fairly.
3. Instill morals, values, and responsibility through manners, chores, duties, etc.
4. Prepare food for them and feed them.
5. Read to them and help them with their homework.
6. Be respectful and courteous with my employers and their children.
7. Make sure the kids have equal time alone with mom and dad so they could bond with their parents.
8. Treat the entire family as if they were my own family.

After what seems like an eternity on the bus, I finally catch a glimpse of the ocean. As we turn onto Pacific Coast Highway, the coastline of Malibu stretches to the left and the right for miles. Huge beach homes sit one after another, literally right on the beach. They are so close to each other, I imagine the neighbors reaching from one window to the next to shake hands. Palm trees are everywhere. Sand, surf, and beautiful, blue skies — Malibu is gorgeous. I sigh. I might be living and working right here. Heaven.

I have no idea how long the bus ride will take, and begin to realize that I haven't given myself nearly enough time. With no way to get in touch with Linda, I say a little prayer and hope she will be at home when I arrive.

When I step off the bus near Linda's house, it is well past my scheduled interview time. Linda lives on the east side of Pacific Coast Highway (which I just learned from my bus driver is called PCH by the locals), across from the beach in a fairly large home surrounded by trees and shrubs. You can't even see the house from the driveway. I feel extremely awkward as I walk down the driveway and push the call button on the intercom that is obviously intended only for cars. I bet they don't have too many people walking down the driveway. The maid answers and buzzes me in. The house is blue with white trim and four times bigger than even the largest home in Norcross. In front of the home is a swimming pool and jacuzzi lined with rocks instead of cement, so they look like naturally formed ponds. Behind the pool is a guesthouse that is as big as my parents' house back home. I can't wait to tell my family how beautiful Malibu is, and about the size of this house, and the location right across from the ocean. They are not going to believe this, I think, as I knock on the front door.

The maid greets me, and says that Linda isn't home. Between her limited English and my two years of Spanish classes, I am able to explain why I am there. She brings me inside to call Linda, who apparently gave up waiting for me, and went to get her hair done.

"Hello. May I help you?" the receptionist at the salon answers.

"Yes. I was wondering if Linda Jenner is there?" I ask.

"Yes she is. Would you like to talk to her?" she questions.

"That would be great. Thank you."

"Hello?" A sweet southern voice coos into the phone.

"Linda. Hi! This is Pam. I'm so sorry. I had to ride the bus to your house, and it took much longer than I thought. I'm here at your house."

I am so embarrassed and think I must be making a horrible first impression. Being late for an appointment is not going to win me any points.

"No problem, honey. Could you come here to the salon? It's just a couple miles away in downtown Malibu. We could talk while I get my hair done."

She says this as if it is the simplest thing in the world, obviously forgetting already that I had taken a bus.

"Sure. I'll be there as soon as I can," I assure her, having no idea how quickly I can get there. I can only hope that her hair appointment takes a *long* time.

I walk back out to the bus stop on PCH, and fortunately, a southbound bus comes by shortly thereafter. As the bus drives into Malibu, I am surprised by what I see. I had expected something like a Sandals/Club Med type of resort, fancy and upscale, with white beaches and lots of glamour. Instead, Malibu is a simple little beach town — casual, understated, and laid back. Most of the businesses are housed in small cottages. After checking the address, and yelling to the bus driver to stop, I find the correct building.

The hair salon is in one of the little cottages painted blue with white trim. I notice from the signs that the salon is on the second floor in the back. I walk up a flight of stairs at the side of the building and become concerned about my outfit, as I wonder if I am dressed appropriately for this meeting. I quickly look over my outfit — the same lovely white shirt-dress from Avon I'd worn at the nanny agency, along with the denim purse, and "I Love Elvis" pin. It worked for the first interview. It will have to do.

The salon is very understated, with only six booths. It seems to me it would fit better in Norcross than Malibu. Linda sits in a salon chair with a cape around her neck, wet hair hanging around her face. She and a hairdresser laugh and chat as if they are good girlfriends. Even with wet hair and dressed in a cape with an awful flower pattern, Linda is obviously very beautiful.

"So you must be Pam," she exclaims in her charming Southern accent, as she sees me walk in.

We chat for some time as she questions me about my background and babysitting experiences. Things are going well, I surmise. She is friendly and nice, and doesn't seem pretentious or condescending, which is a pleasant surprise.

She notices my purse pin and asks, "So you like Elvis?"

I respond, "Oh yeah! How about you?"

"Well I better," she replies. "I lived with him for four years."

I start to laugh, certain that she is teasing me.

The gal that is doing Linda's hair turns my laugh into a gasp by telling me, "She's not kidding!"

I can't believe it. I stand there for a moment with my mouth hanging open, not quite knowing what to say. I remember how I cried the day Elvis died, and how much I loved his music. Now here I am interviewing with his former girlfriend. Questions pop up in my head. I have so many things I want to ask her about Elvis.

All I can muster is, "No way!"

"Yes, it's true. And I can tell by your face that you obviously really like him too."

I have found my voice again.

"Oh yes, I LOVE Elvis! I had a record player, and I used to play his records over and over. That is so cool that you were his girlfriend. Wow. I have so many questions for you," I exclaim.

"I'm sure you do," Linda smiles, but then continues, "but first, I have some questions for you."

I remember I am actually here for an interview.

"Oh yes, I'm sorry. Of course. Ask me whatever you would like," I respond sheepishly.

She invites me to sit down in the empty salon chair next to her, and we chat for about thirty minutes. By the time I leave the salon, Linda has offered me the job as nanny for her two boys, Brandon (who is seven) and Brody (who is almost five). I really think that silly little Elvis pin cemented the job for me.

What a day — Malibu, the beach, a new job, and Elvis's girlfriend. I can't wait to see what will happen next.

MALIBU NANNY

June 15, 1988
Dear, Dear, Dear, Dad and Ma,

Yesterday was Father's Day and I worked at JCPenneys all day. Can you believe that they don't have any Dairy Queens out here? That really gets my goat!

I haven't heard anything from Linda lately because she's in Nashville. I'm really excited about going to Linda's. I must admit, as the time gets closer, I'm getting kinda scared. I just keep thinking something will go wrong and she won't want me. I guess I'll just have to wait and see.

Well, I gotta go back to Nickels, I mean Penneys. Please take good care of yourselves and always remember how much I love your darling faces.

I love U & Miss U,
Pam

CHAPTER THREE
Breakfast of Champions

My first day of work is the Fourth of July. Linda asks me to arrive in the early evening. I pack up my belongings in my one little suitcase, say goodbye to Sara, and hop back on the bus for the long ride from Pasadena to Malibu. My mind is filled with questions. What are Brandon and Brody like? Will they accept me? Linda seemed really sweet, but how will she be as a boss? I can't wait to ask her about Elvis, and hope she won't mind talking about him. I want to know every detail of her time with him.

When I arrive, only the maid is home. Since we can't converse well, and she has things to do, I am left alone to wait for Linda and the boys to arrive. After twenty minutes of waiting, I become impatient and begin to wander around the house. In the huge living room (which is decorated in a country floral motif) sits an upright piano. I want to play it, but wonder if that would be appropriate. I should probably ask permission first. I wait for ten more minutes, and still no one arrives. Finally, I sit down and play. Anxious and nervous about meeting Brandon and Brody, I play and sing to keep my nerves from going haywire. I only know a couple of songs from memory — Music Box Dancer and Fur Elise. I play both pieces, and then thumb through a book of piano music lying on top of the piano. I pick out a few tunes, and continue playing.

I take in my surroundings, including the many pictures that are in frames on the walls, desks and tables. One frame after another, I see the face of Bruce Jenner staring back at me. Linda "Jenner." It hadn't even crossed my mind as a possibility before, but now I begin to realize who I might be working for — none other than Bruce Jenner, Olympic decathlon champion.

I started eating Wheaties, "the Breakfast of Champions," for breakfast when I was still in elementary school. As I became involved in sports in high school, I never missed my bowl of Wheaties, knowing they were making me stronger and faster. Many mornings, I sat in my chair, staring at the face of Bruce Jenner on the front of the Wheaties box. I thought he was so cute. He was an American hero, because he won the gold medal in the most challenging sports event in the Olympics during America's Centennial year of 1976. My dad praised him constantly as the epitome of a true all around sports champion, and he became an icon in my household.

Now here I am in his house. I can't believe it. Butterflies flit around my stomach, and I actually feel light headed. I begin to wonder when and how I will meet him. Linda had told me she was divorced. I wonder if he is a big part of the boys' lives. Does he come over to Linda's house often? I imagine how nervous I will be when I finally meet him. Oh my gosh, what will I wear?

When the front door opens around seven p.m., the boys blow in like a tornado, full of energy and excitement. I am expecting to see Linda right behind them, but to my great surprise, it is Bruce Jenner himself. My idol, the American Hero, the man on the Wheaties box. Here he is standing right in front of me. Flabbergasted, nervous, excited, shocked, overwhelmed — I am a jumble of emotions.

He extends his hand and says, "I'm Bruce. This is Brandon, and this is Brody."

"Hi, I'm Pam," I stammer, shell shocked and unprepared to meet my idol so soon.

Immediately, I realize that Bruce is down to earth and friendly, and within moments I feel comfortable with him. Bruce looks exactly like the man I'd seen so many times on television and in the newspaper. He is dressed very casually, in a t-shirt, shorts, and tennis shoes. He looks much taller than I had expected and has a lean, athletic build. His hair is cut and styled the same way I'd seen in every image of him — a little bit long, straight as can be, and a bit unkempt, as if he'd just finished a run.

The boys are incredibly cute, but full of energy. They run circles through the rooms in the house. They are a blur, pumped up from their fourth of July celebration. I wonder to myself if they are also nervous to meet their new nanny. They finally stop long enough to say hi to me.

Brandon has sun bleached light brown hair, brown eyes, and seems tall for a seven year old. He has the same lean, athletic build of his father. Brody's hair is a bit darker, and he also has brown eyes that reflect a mischievous personality. His build is a bit more muscular than his older brother.

After a few minutes of chatting with me, Bruce says, "Okay, I'll be leaving the boys with you now. Linda should be home soon."

I am more than a little nervous about the prospect of being alone with these little men at the moment. Bruce must see the distress in my eyes, as he announces he will stay for a little while until the boys calm down. Eventually Brandon and Brody settle down, and I help Bruce put them to bed.

After the boys are asleep, Bruce and I sit in the living room, and he asks me some questions about life in Minnesota and why I chose to move to

Los Angeles. He is easy to talk to, for which I am thankful. I still feel a bit star struck, but his easygoing personality makes me relax. We talk for about twenty minutes, and then he says he is going to head home.

As he heads out the front door, he turns around with a big smile on his face, and says, "You'll be seeing a lot of me."

I sure hope so.

Possibilities float through my head. Linda and Bruce are divorced. I'm single. He is a very handsome man, not to mention my childhood hero. I recognize the feelings of a crush beginning to form, but push the thoughts aside with rational considerations. He's the ex-husband of your boss. He must be twice your age.

My thoughts turn to the two little boys who will now be my responsibility. Although I had several years of babysitting experience with Nicholas and Katie, this is a whole new ball game. Two boys, close in age, with an obviously high energy level. I utter a little prayer.

"God, help me do a good job."

CHAPTER FOUR
The Beauty Queen

A short time later, Linda arrives home. With her long, blonde hair blow dried out, she looks even more beautiful than the woman I met in the hair salon. She is tall and slender, with long, lean legs that make her seem even taller. My girlfriends and I have always complained about our thighs, hoping we could somehow work out enough or diet enough to lose our "thick thighs" and look like the models in the magazines. Linda has thin thighs just like those models. I feel both admiration and jealousy.

There are so many things I could and should ask her, but honestly, all I can think about is Elvis. I can't wait to hear about Elvis.

We sit on the floral sofa in her living room that night and talk for hours. She is down to earth, sweet, funny, and I honestly feel like I am talking to an older sister. I love her immediately.

She has many questions about my family, my hometown, and life in Minnesota. Although she lives an affluent life now, Linda's background was much like mine. We are both country girls at heart.

Linda shares that she was born in the South, which I surmised from her accent. She grew up in Memphis, Tennessee. In her teenage years, she became a beauty queen and won many titles. I am not surprised given her beauty.

I am even more impressed when she tells me that she placed third in the Miss Tennessee pageant (part of the Miss America pageant).

"So how did you meet Elvis?" I ask, when I can hold out no longer.

She laughs. I'm sure she has been expecting the question.

"I was twenty-two years old, and I met him at a theater in Memphis."

She regales me with stories of her four years as Elvis's girlfriend, and I listen, fascinated, hanging on every word. I can't believe I am now working for the former girlfriend of my first love. And the ex-wife of my childhood hero. Things like this don't happen to a girl from Norcross, Minnesota.

I think about these two men, so different in many ways. Elvis was a rock star — one of the biggest rock stars who ever lived. Bruce was the other end of the spectrum — a jock, arguably one of the best all around athletes ever. But they shared one trait — they were both American heroes, loved and praised by millions, the best in their field. It says a lot about Linda — her beauty, her kind heart, her sweetness — and her ability to captivate them. I begin to feel a kinship with her, because I also adored these two men.

Although the boys each have separate rooms, Linda tells me that Brandon always sleeps in Brody's room in the bunk beds, because they are both afraid of the dark and like to be together. My first night as a nanny, I sleep in Brandon's room, in a bed shaped like a 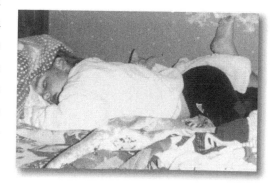 racecar. The walls have Crayola color crayons stuck to them. They are like big art boards the boys can draw on. I pick up a crayon and draw two big hearts, and write "Brandon" in one and "Brody" in the other.

On one side of the room is a loft, filled with toys and games. A fantasy room for a little boy. I'm not a little boy, however, so it does feel a little strange to be sleeping in a racecar, surrounded by toys. I don't let it bother me too much, because I really had no expectations about my sleeping arrangement. Linda and I never talked about it, but of course, it doesn't feel like *my* room.

I'm thankful that another member of the family has chosen to sleep near me on the floor — the Golden Lab named Louie. He is a huge, mellow, good-natured mound of yellow fur, and we take to each other quickly. We had a black lab named King when I was young, so having a lab around helps me feel at home.

Linda told me earlier that evening how she and Bruce divorced in 1984 when the boys were still just toddlers. Bruce lives only a few miles away and is actively involved in their lives. She told me that they have agreed Bruce would spend time with the boys at Linda's house rather than shuttle them between two homes.

Although the divorce wasn't recent, I imagine the boys still suffer the emotional upheaval from the separation of their parents. Add to that the adjustment of a total stranger in their home who is now their nanny, and I realize the transition may be difficult.

As I fall asleep that night, I attempt to put myself in their shoes and imagine how hard it is for these two little boys to acclimate to someone new in their life. I don't know anything about the previous nanny, and I have been hesitant to ask. I know it must be hard to trust and love again — hard to believe that the next nanny is not going to leave. I make a commitment to myself that I am going to make this work. I don't want to hurt those boys.

As I expected, my first few weeks as nanny to the Jenner boys are emotional and challenging at times, as it is a transition period for all of us. It certainly is quite an adjustment for me. I thought I was emotionally prepared for this and up to the task since I had babysat Nicholas and Katie for years. I realize it is very different when you are in charge of kids on a full time basis. With babysitting, it was usually a few hours here and there. Really, when I think about it, my main responsibility was to play with them. Also, Nicholas and Katie were almost four years apart. Brandon and Brody are only two years apart, and are super high-energy boys. I spend a lot of time playing with them as well, but there is so much more to it. Breakfast, clothing changes, practice, school, lunch, homework, dinner, bedtime, managing their fights, and setting down and enforcing rules.

I'm very thankful that I was a tomboy and active in sports. I can dive in and do what the boys are doing, whether it's jumping on the trampoline, running, playing catch, or fishing. I'm not grossed out easily, and I don't worry about bumps, bruises or scratches.

Not long after I start working for Linda, she comes home from the gym one day and says, "Sylvester Stallone asked me out. Do you think I should go?"

"Oh my gosh," I stammer, "of course you should go."

I can't believe she is even considering *not* going out with him.

Sly, as I like to call him, became my second great love, after Elvis. My relationship with Sly blossomed in a movie theater while watching *Rambo II* in 1985. Mesmerized by him, I rented every movie he'd ever been in, and watched them over and over, fantasizing about marrying him some day. I could quote all his lines, word for word. I imagined having little boys that looked exactly like Sly running around. I'd name them Rocky and Rambo. If we had a girl, I'd call her Adrian.

My high school locker was covered with posters and pictures of Sly, and all of my classmates and friends knew I loved him. I talked about him constantly. My favorite song was "Eye of the Tiger" from *Rocky III*. My friends would cut out pictures of him for me, and draw hearts that said "Pam and Sly forever" on pieces of notepaper, and slip them to me during class. I even dated a boy named Jamie, who was four years younger than me, simply because he looked like Sylvester Stallone. We used to go roller-skating together. I'd drive to the rink, and his mom would drop him off. When you're in your twenties or beyond, four years is not a big deal, but when you are a senior girl in high school, dating an eighth grade boy is taboo. I was called "cradle robber" many times, but I didn't care. I just imagined myself kissing Sly every time I kissed Jamie. I was obsessed, to put it lightly.

Linda explains that Sly goes to the same gym as her, and they have become friends. I am slightly jealous, but it's not like *I* could date him. She is gorgeous and in his league. I am not. I realize I can live vicariously through her, and I might even get to meet him.

After she agrees to go out with him, I am giddy with excitement and beg her to let me answer the door when he shows up for one of their dates. This is the adventure and excitement I was hoping for when I moved to Los Angeles for the summer. I can't believe I may meet not just your everyday celebrity, but a megastar, who happens to be the man of my dreams.

July 21, 1988
Dear Mom & Dad,

Last weekend, Sara and I went to Rambo III starring SYLVESTER STALLONE. I can't believe I might get to meet him! I guess there is a God in heaven! Ha! Yo dad! Yo Mom! Take her easy!

I Love You,
Pammy

As I begin to fantasize about meeting Stallone, the reality of my life as a nanny becomes clear. I feel like I have been forced into adulthood. Here I am nineteen years old, with a prior life of school, sports, and partying at college. I had never faced any real responsibility. Now, I have taken a job of running a household, being a grown up, and watching over two young boys. Wow. It is a reality check. So this is what it is like to be an adult. I'm not sure I want all of this. But I'm not a quitter, and I want to be faithful and loyal to this family — to Linda, to Bruce, and to these two little boys I've chosen to take care of and love. So I will not give up.

I am in awe of the celebrities I work for and interact with, the Malibu lifestyle, the nice cars, and the life of the rich and famous. Both Linda and Bruce drive white Porsches, and Bruce also has a white Thunderbird. I drive a classy, 1970's era, station wagon that has wood paneling on its sides. I feel like Alice from the Brady Bunch whenever I drive that beast. I own only three cassette tapes — Madonna, the Beach Boys, and Def Leppard — so I listen to them over and over. It doesn't take long for the boys to have every song memorized.

As Bruce promised me that first night I met him, I do see a lot of him. He comes by almost every day. I ask Linda what the custody arrangement is, and she tells me they don't really have anything official. He has freedom to come and go as he pleases, and to be a regular part of their life. Linda and Bruce have committed to having a friendly relationship for the sake of the boys. I am impressed that they have been able to put aside their differences and make their children the priority. It is clear to me that the boys love their mom and dad very much and have close, sweet relationships with both of them.

Since his time in the Olympics, Bruce has done a great deal of motivational public speaking, which doesn't surprise me, because he is one of the most positive people I have ever met. He travels fairly often to give speeches around the country, but when he is home, he's over at Linda's house regularly. Occasionally, he takes the boys to his house, but he seems to be quite comfortable at Linda's (which makes sense since he lived there for many years). He mentions to me that he wants the boys to be in the same house most of the time and doesn't want them to have to go back and forth.

Bruce often picks the boys up from school, and then the four of us work on homework together, take the boys to T-ball or soccer practice and games, cook dinner together, grab some ice cream, or go out to eat. When the boys are with him, Bruce doesn't expect me to be the primary caregiver. He is a fully present parent. He takes care of them and doles out discipline as necessary. It is an opportunity for me to just have fun and enjoy their company.

Occasionally, Bruce's kids from his first marriage join us on outings. His son, Burt, is eleven, and his daughter, Casey, is nine. They are sweet, kind kids and get along well with Brandon and Brody.

I am actually surprised how seamlessly Linda and Bruce manage their time with the kids and their relationship. There is no drama. They spend fairly equal amounts of time with the boys. They each have time when one of them is gone for work obligations, and the other one picks up the slack. It all just works.

I've become very fond of Bruce. He is like a big brother to me, and has become a dear friend. I had a bit of a crush to begin with, but we've settled into a comfortable friendship, and I'm happy with that. First of all, anything else would be inappropriate, but secondly, I really love him as a person and I wouldn't want to do anything that would ruin our friendship.

One night in mid August, Bruce picks up the boys and takes us to his house to watch the opening ceremony for the 1988 Olympic games. We stop at the grocery store, and he picks out ingredients for dinner. He makes a delicious pasta dish with spinach noodles, broccoli, and zucchini, covered in red sauce. After dinner, we watch part of the opening ceremony, and then "ooh" and "ahh" as the broadcast shows highlights of Bruce's Olympic performances.

I share with him a story from *my* athletic career. I still have nightmares about one track meet. My coach decides on the day of a meet that I should run the 330-meter hurdles. I had *never* run that race before, not even in practice. It is one of the toughest races, as you have to sprint through the entire race, and 330 meters is a long way to sprint. I wanted to cry, felt like throwing up, and almost walked off the track to have my dad take me home. But I didn't want to let my team down, so I agreed to try. I did okay for the first few hurdles, but then I saw the girl in front of me fall down. Usually if someone falls down in a sprint race, it's guaranteed that you will beat her. Not me. She got up and still beat me. I've never been so embarrassed and humiliated in my entire life.

As I finish my story, Bruce grimaces and utters in a pained voice, "Don't *ever* tell that story again in *my* house." Not in the house of a decathlon champion. He is kidding of course…or is he?

One night we are chatting as we go about our usual routine — homework, dinner, getting the kids ready for bed.

"Pam, I have to tell you something that will surprise you."

"Oh, what's that?" I ask, expecting a joke, because he is *always* joking with me.

"I am dyslexic."

He tells me how he overcame dyslexia as a child. He went on to explain that his athletic career began, not in track and field, but in football. He played football in high school and actually earned a football scholarship to attend Graceland College in Iowa. Unfortunately, a knee injury forced him to quit, and he switched to the decathlon.

"Thank goodness for that, or I wouldn't have been staring at you on the Wheaties box for all those years," I tease.

He grins widely.

"I have one more," Bruce announces.

"One more what?" I ask, having no clue what he is referring to.

"One more thing about me that will surprise you."

"Really? What?"

"I used to play the accordion," Bruce admits, grinning from ear to ear.

Bruce actually does have a musical side to him. Soon after, Bruce asks me to give him piano lessons. We spend many hours side by side at the piano when the boys are at school during the day. I give Bruce simple songs to practice. He also likes to listen to me play. One of our favorite

songs is the theme from the movie, *Beaches,* titled "Wind Beneath my Wings." I play and we both sing as loud as we possibly can. I love it because the lyrics are, "Did you ever know that you're my hero?" And Bruce *was* my hero, so it is fun to sing that line to him, as he sits next to me on the piano bench.

Bruce owns a small plane and has a pilot's license. In August, Bruce flies the boys and me up to Lake Tahoe, where his father lives. Bruce owns a cabin. It is nothing fancy, but right on the lake, cozy, and comfortable. I have so much fun as Bruce teaches me how to jet ski, water ski, and play golf. I consider myself a fairly well rounded athlete, but these sports are all new to me. Brandon and Brody have already advanced far beyond me, so it is a little bit intimidating.

Learning to water ski on Lake Tahoe is a torturous process. The lake is about fifteen hundred feet deep, so it never warms up. Even in the middle of summer, the water is freezing.

We take a boat out on the lake. With his father driving, Bruce shows me how it's done. He grew up water skiing and is a pro. While Brandon, Brody, and I watch in amazement, Bruce does tricks, flips, and turns. He drops one ski, and skis "slalom style" on one ski. Then he drops both skis and water skis with just his bare feet.

Finally, it's my turn. I am quite hesitant, but Bruce is insistent that I try. He jumps in the water with me, and shows me how to lean back and let the boat pull me up.

"Don't try too hard. Let the boat do the work for you."

Brandon and Brody already know how to water ski, and it is added pressure that they are in the boat watching. Bruce jumps in the boat, takes the wheel, and starts the engine.

I give him the thumbs up sign, as he instructed. The boat takes off, and I'm waiting for the line to become taut. I hear the boys yelling.

"Come on, Pam! You can do it, Pam! "

The line tightens, and I try to remember Bruce's instructions. I grip the handle, and the line pulls me up, and I immediately fall sideways into the water.

Bruce comes around again for another try.

"You can do it, Pam," he yells. "Remember, let the boat do the work for you."

I try again. And again. And again.

After numerous falls, I am pretty much done, and resign myself to the fact that I may never learn how to water ski. However, I work for a decathlon champion, who doesn't understand the words "I can't." He knows only "I

can" and, consequently, "you can" and "you will." He won't let me give up until I have mastered it. It takes about ten tries, but finally I am up and skiing. The boys scream with excitement.

The lake is crystal clear, and we are the only boat on the water. Skiing around the lake is a thrilling experience. I feel like I am gliding over the water. I've always loved the water, and this is so much fun. I almost feel as though the real world doesn't exist. It is a wonderful escape from the routine back in Malibu.

On the return flight, I watch the boys interacting with their father and contemplate my first month with them. Despite my up and down emotions, I have begun to adjust to my life as a nanny, and the boys are learning they can trust me. We are becoming best buddies. I am falling in love with them, and they with me. Despite my fears and some initial challenges of adapting to one another, I am pleased that we are bonding so well.

Both boys are cute, precocious, and full of energy, like any normal boys. Brandon loves to sit on my shoulders and wants me to carry him around all over, while he pretends that he is really tall. He is a natural athlete like his dad, and loves all sports. I call him "stud muffin." One day the previous week, Brandon rode his skateboard down a hill on his stomach. He was going so fast, I was scared that he would crash and get hurt. He is a real daredevil. I imagine that Brandon will follow in his father's footsteps and be a star athlete someday, because he excels in every sport he tries.

Brody is also athletic, but his passion is nature. He is always chasing hummingbirds, butterflies, squirrels, chipmunks, and bees around the yard or in the outfield at T-Ball practice. Brody loves sunglasses, and often grabs Linda's or mine and poses, asking us to take a picture of him. I imagine Brody will either be a park ranger so he can be in the great outdoors or a celebrity, since he loves to have his picture taken so much.

One day, Brandon decides he is not going to T-Ball practice. He takes off running across the yard. I chase right after him. Brandon turns around, and his shocked expression shows his disbelief that I am right behind him. He trips and falls, and the race is over. He goes to T-Ball without further incident.

Both boys love to fish at a local man made pond called TroutDale that is stocked with fish. We rent bamboo fishing rods, purchase kernels of corn and "fish" for hours. I feel bad for the boys, wishing they could fish the way I did growing up — in a boat, on a huge lake, catching wild fish, not these tiny stocked in a small, manmade pond. One day, I tell them the story about the big fish I caught as a little girl, and their eyes grow wide in amazement.

Fishing was a way of life for my family. From the time I was very small, we went on fishing trips together. For years, my Dad had been hearing that the state record Walleye came out of Saganaga Lake up in the boundary waters area on the border of Minnesota and Canada. When I was eleven years old, we took a family fishing trip up there and stayed on an island in Saganaga Lake. We took a boat from the mainland to the island, where we stayed in rustic cabins without running water. We arrived in early evening, and my Dad insisted that we jump in the boat immediately and go out and fish "just for a little bit."

So I'm sitting in the boat, with a fishing pole in my hand, the line trailing in the water off to the side of the boat, not paying much attention to anything but the M&M's I was eating. I felt a tug on my pole.

"Oh Dad, I'm snagged on something," I complained, hoping he'd unhook it for me, so I could get back to my M&M's.

My father looked at the line intently.

"The hell you are. You better start reeling that in!" my father bellowed.

"Oh my gosh!" I screamed, as M&M's flew everywhere while I tried to take command of my pole.

I reeled in my catch, and as the fish surfaced above the water, our mouths dropped open as we saw before us the biggest Walleye we'd ever laid eyes on. I thought my dad was going to have a heart attack, and my brother almost fell overboard as he rushed to help me.

The cabin resort where we were staying didn't have a formal weighing device, so we had to wait until morning to take the boat into the mainland to weigh the monster. My prize Walleye weighed ten pounds and thirteen ounces. That week I won the fishing contest in Minnesota.

A couple of years later, my Dad went back to the same lake and caught a ten pound, six ounce Walleye in the exact same spot. Our prize fish are mounted facing each other at my mom's home in Minnesota.

As I finish my story, and hold up my hands to show the boys exactly how big my prize walleye was, they both exclaim in unison, "No way!" They talk about my fish *every* day for the next two weeks.

CHAPTER FIVE
Awake, Alert, Alive

Each morning, I wake the boys in my own special way. They hate it, but it works. I enter their room, switch on the overhead light, and say "Awake! Alert, alive, and ENTHUUUUUUUSIASTIC!"

I exclaim this in the most positive, chipper, and, I'm sure, annoying voice I can muster at such an early hour. My loud voice, combined with the bright light, does the trick. They moan, groan, and protest, but it *always* gets them up.

At nighttime, we often play a game of Memory, which they both love. Then, I read books (*Goodnight Moon* is one of their favorites), say prayers, and tuck them into bed. Often, right before they fall asleep, we peek at the stars, and the boys love to say "Star light, star bright, first star I see tonight. Wish I may, wish I might, have the wish I wish tonight."

I heard Linda say this one night as we were outside, and she spotted the first star. So now, whether we are outdoors or in their room looking out the window, whoever spots the first star, gets to start, "Star light, star bright..."

We spend countless hours jumping on the trampoline. The boys love to lay or sit on the trampoline, and then I jump as hard as I can right next to them to make them fly high up into the air. We have so much fun, and often end up on our backs, all three of us giggling uncontrollably. The boys have been trying to convince me for a long time to do a front flip on the trampoline. Finally, one day I decide I am going to try it. I muster all of my courage and jump as hard as I can, flip over in the air, land on my feet, and then fall forward onto my hands and knees.

"You did it! You did it!"

Both boys jump on top of me, unable to contain their excitement. We fall in a heap, laughing.

Linda loves to jump on the trampoline with the boys as well. Unfortunately, she breaks her ankle one day as she lands in an awkward position and hobbles around in a bright pink cast for weeks. She wears fuchsia pink toenail polish to match the cast.

Linda and I get along very well — we have from day one. She is a kind and warm-hearted person and genuinely seems to care about me. We laugh a lot.

I am in the kitchen one day laughing with the boys, and Linda pokes her head down the stairway and says with a big grin, "Pam, you have a great laugh! I will *never* forget your laugh."

She jokes a lot and has a great sense of humor. When people compliment her, she holds up both hands, left palm facing out, as in "stop" and the other hand waving in, as in "come on, give me more compliments." I think it's hilarious and begin emulating her.

Linda is still single. She dates here and there and goes out with girlfriends, but most nights she is home fairly early. As we did that first night, she and I often curl up on the couch and chat about life, love, our childhoods, our families, and, of course, Elvis.

She loves to talk about him, and often tells me stories about their time together. She lights up. I'm not sure who is more excited — her talking about him, or me listening to the stories. It is obvious to me from the look on her face, and the way she talks about him all the time, that she still loves Elvis dearly. I come to realize through her stories that they had a very passionate and deep connection, yet he wasn't the best choice for a partner, as she was with him near the end, when drugs played a huge part in his life.

Linda is a great mom. It is obvious she loves the boys very much. She is always affectionate with them — lots of hugs and kisses. They run up to her bed in the morning and cuddle with her. I hear them talking and giggling. They use a hand signal to say, "I love you" — two middle fingers bent, the other three up.

Linda spends a lot of time with her boys. I am invited along when she takes them out for activities, shopping, or to eat. We have many fun outings together — the four of us. Soccer and t-ball games are always a family affair, and we often stop for ice cream on the way home. We also go out to eat several times a week. We all love going to the beach, searching for treasures like sand crabs, sea shells, sand dollars, and jellyfish.

I begin to feel like a member of the family. As a single mom, I think Linda enjoys the companionship of having me around. I like to imagine she thinks of me more as her little sister than her nanny.

Although I do feel like Linda and the boys are my family, and they treat me that way, there is a part of me that is uncomfortable with that recognition. Am I beginning to lose my identity? *Their* life has become *my* life.

After sleeping in Brandon's room for a few months, I get to move to the maid's room, because the live-in maid has left. It is right across from the boys' rooms, has a nice skylight, and is decorated cute and girly, so it feels more like my own.

I realize a nanny's day is never done. My days don't really end until I go to sleep, sometimes not even then. If the boys are sick or have a bad dream during the night, they come and crawl into bed with me. It's sweet to know they feel that way about me, but it's hard sometimes, because then it's not really my own time. It becomes a round-the-clock job.

The boys are at school during the day and when Linda is gone, I feel very lonely. I have no friends other than the boys, Linda, and Bruce. It is also boring, with not a whole lot to do. The isolation starts to affect me.

Before I took this job, I spent a month with Sara and got used to her constant companionship. Before that, I was in college with three roommates. I was also on the volleyball team and worked at a restaurant, so I had regular social interaction with kids my age. Now, I work all the time, and on my time off, I don't have a car (or anywhere to go if I did), so I spend my day off alone in my room.

Sara lives in an apartment near USC, which is about forty minutes away. She has a serious boyfriend and spends most of her spare time with him. We are both very busy, so it is hard to spend time together. Occasionally, she drives out to Malibu and spends a night with me and vice versa.

One weekend, I ask Linda if I can drive the station wagon to USC on my day off. She agrees, and I have a fun weekend in the dorm with Sara, pretending I'm in school again. It is so nice to be around kids my age, in a social environment. It highlights how isolated I am at the Jenner home and makes me think about college again.

I had initially planned to take just the summer off, but by the time I started working at Linda's, the summer was half over, so I told my parents I'd take a year off, and then head back to college next fall. I wonder now, as I see the bustle of life on the USC campus, if I made the right decision.

I'm thankful when Linda asks me to run errands for her, like grocery shopping. Going to the grocery store in Malibu (although it sounds like a routine, boring assignment) is quite exciting. Before I leave, I put on makeup and choose the cutest outfit I can find, because I never know who I might run into at the store. Larry Hagman of *Dallas* fame, Mel Gibson, Linda Hamilton from *The Terminator*, Bruce Willis, Michael Landon, Pat Benatar, and Johnny Carson are some of the famous faces I shop with at the local market.

For a small town girl, it is quite an experience just to walk through the grocery store, which is twenty times bigger than any we had back home, with dim lighting and chandeliers, and exotic fruits I have never heard of before.

One day, as I pick out the boys' favorite cheese, I look up and there is Farrah Fawcett next to me examining a block of cheese. I have learned to hide my reactions, because by now, sighting stars has become a regular occurrence, so I turn around quickly, and push my cart away. When I am a decent distance away, I turn around and gawk at her, amazed to see the star I'd admired for years on Charlie's Angels.

I befriend the new maid, Millie. To alleviate my boredom, I even offer to help her out with some of her chores. We laugh and joke together. She teaches me some Spanish, and we eat lunch together regularly. Other than the family I work for, she is my only constant friendship.

It's a sweltering morning in September (two months since I started this job), and I'm feeling sad, lonely and really quite sorry for myself. I walk to the mailbox, and my spirits lift as I spot the familiar, elegant cursive writing — a letter from home. My mom and dad have become my lifeline, as I cope with the reality of my lonely life as a nanny. I talk to them a couple times each week on the phone. (Linda pays for my phone calls, as long as I don't abuse the privilege, which I appreciate so much.) But my parents and I still send letters back and forth, and I always look forward to getting them. They make me a bit homesick. Everything back home seems to be the way it was, and everyone is happy and healthy. I guess there is a part of me that wishes they weren't quite so okay without me.

September 16, 1988
Dear Daddy & Ma,

Thank you so much for the pictures. The boys flipped when they saw how big that Halibut was. I can't believe the size of that monster.

Poor Louie has fleas so bad that he has bitten a whole section of his tail off. Eeeek!!!!! There's a humongous spider in my room! It might be a Black Widow!! OK. Relax. I just killed him and I still have goose bumps. Yuck! They're almost as bad as grasshoppers.

School is going great for the boys. I dress them so cute every day. The other day little Brody had to be vaccinated with a shot in the butt. Linda, Brandon and I took him to the doctor and we all went in with him. His face looked so scared and I was so worried for him that I had tears in my eyes. He didn't even cry though. Brandon held his hand.

Linda promised that next week would be the week I get to meet Stallone so I'm starting to get ready now. Ha! No, I'm kidding. But I am going to get my hair layered all over. I'm sick of it long on top. So I hope it looks all right. Haircuts are outrageous here. The cheapest you can get is about $15.00.

I love you and miss you,
Pammy Jean

At the end of September, I have a day off, and ask Linda if I can borrow the station wagon to go to visit Sara and her boyfriend in Pasadena. She agrees, and I jump on the freeway to begin the forty-five minute drive. About twenty minutes into the drive, I notice a white Porsche in the distance pulled off to the side of the road. It peaks my interest because both Linda and Bruce own white Porsches, and they are not that common. I signal and change lanes several times, so that I am in the far right lane. As I get closer, I realize — to my great surprise — it is Bruce, so I pull over to help him. He is startled to see me. Imagine the odds. It's not like I was right around the corner from Linda's house in Malibu. I chalk it up to serendipity.

I realize one day that Bruce is my first truly platonic male friendship. He hasn't tried to date me or sleep with me. We have a lot in common, including a shared birthday. We were both born on October 28, nineteen years apart. I tease him that he is twice my age. We laugh, joke, talk about our lives, and enjoy the time we spend with the boys. Bruce has become a dear friend.

CHAPTER SIX
My Sly

I finally get my chance to meet Sly. He is planning to come by the house to pick up Linda for a date. I am excited, nervous, scared, and breathless with anticipation. Peeking out the window from behind a curtain, I watch him pull up in a sleek, black Jaguar. He steps out of the car, sporting a bright colorful Hawaiian shirt and some very tight jeans. Oh my. With his bronzed skin, aviator sunglasses, and a wooden matchstick in his mouth, he is ultra cool, wealthy, powerful, and gorgeous. He looks exactly how you would expect a mega star to look. He is far more handsome in person. My heart is doing somersaults, and the sands in the hourglass stop midair.

I push back the curtain so he won't catch me gawking at him and then wait for him to knock. When he does, I pause a few moments so it's not obvious I am waiting right behind the door, and then open it. As I look into his face, Sylvester Stallone's presence, the scent of his cologne, and the gaze of his dark brown eyes wash over me in waves, and I am utterly mesmerized by this man I have been in love with for years. My mouth is hanging open, and I stand there with the door handle in my grip, staring.

And then he speaks — in that famous, low, gravelly voice.

"Yo Adrian!"

Oh no, that's not what he said, although that's what I hear in my brain, which is now complete mush. Is this really happening? Am I really here talking to Sylvester Stallone?

I realize he is standing there waiting for me to respond. I don't know what he actually said, but assume it was something along the lines of, "Hello is Linda here?" Although I'm not sure because I am in my own crazy little world. But I must say something.

"Oh just a moment, I'll get her for you," I manage, and turn around and retreat inside, leaving him standing in the doorway. (I kick myself for not inviting him in, or saying hello, or introducing myself.)

I peek out the window again, as Sly holds the door of his car open for Linda, and watch as they drive away, wishing it was me on a date with him.

Linda and Sly start seeing each other fairly regularly. He calls the house for her often, and thankfully, I get the chance to redeem myself, and tell him my name. We have short, friendly conversations before I run to get Linda. His voice always gets to me.

One day, Linda confides in me about something.

"Pam, I have a confession to make."

"Oh, what's that?" I ask.

"I told Sly that you have a huge crush on him," she admits.

"Linda! Oh my gosh. Why did you do that? I am so embarrassed," I feign.

The truth is I am secretly overjoyed. Maybe if he knows I like him, he'll talk to me longer or tease me about it.

One afternoon, Sly calls, and chats with me longer than usual. After talking for a while, he still hasn't inquired about Linda, so I ask, "Did you call for Linda?"

He replies, "No I called for you."

What? I am confused and not sure what is going on. We continue to chat for a while. When I get off the phone with him, my stomach is churning. I am flattered, excited, and on a high because Sly has shown interest in me, but also confused. What is going on with Linda and him? I thought they were dating. Have things changed? I am very confused.

When Linda gets home that night, I tell her that Sly called to speak with me. She is upset and tells me they recently broke up. It dawns on me that he is playing games, trying to make Linda jealous. I assume it is a game that will be short-lived and expect that I won't hear from him again.

However, Sly begins to call me quite regularly during times when he assumes Linda won't be home, and asks me to go out with him. I make it clear that I know he is using me to try to make Linda jealous. However, I rationalize my conversations with him, telling myself there's nothing wrong with this because Linda broke up with him. It is too hard for me to say, I can't talk to you. I am torn. I don't want to lose my job, but I don't want to lose him either. This is an unbelievable dream come true. I make a choice to take a risk — to live an adventure — even though I know my decision may have negative ramifications.

Eventually, after the excitement and flattery of having Sly pursuing me wears off a bit, I tell him one day that going behind her back is not acceptable, and I am not going to play games. I tell him that I absolutely will not go out with him. As I speak the words, my brain screams, Did you just say no to Sylvester Stallone? Are you crazy?

Despite the fact they've broken up, I know this could hurt me down the line, and I don't want to lose my job. I don't want to be disloyal to Linda or do anything to hurt her.

Not one to be dissuaded, Sly does not take no for an answer. He knows by now how much I like him, and how obsessed with him I have been (because I told him). I guess he figures he'll wear me down eventually, so he keeps calling, and I talk to him. Occasionally, I feel really guilty and tell him I don't want to talk to him anymore.

But he keeps calling, and eventually I relent and talk to him. It is *Sylvester Stallone.* I'm just not that strong or that good I guess. I can't dismiss his interest in me. I'm sure I represent a challenge to him. How many women tell him no? Not many, I'm betting. I have no friends outside of the Jenner family and the maid, and this is Sylvester Stallone, the mega movie star and the man of my dreams with whom I've been infatuated since I was fourteen years old, and he is interested in *me.*

He continues to ask me to go on a date with him, and I continually say no. The truth is, I'm scared to death. I doubt I can meet his expectations. He has been with many beautiful women. I don't feel good about myself. I'm not thin. I'm constantly battling my weight, trying to stay on a diet and lose some pounds, but I always fail.

One day, he calls and asks me out yet again, and I decide to be honest with him.

"Sly, no I can't go out with you. The truth is I'm scared," I finally admit.

"What do you mean? What are you scared of?" he asks in that low, husky voice.

"I don't think I will live up to your expectations. You have dated so many beautiful women. I can't live up to that," I say, nervous about how he will react.

"Pam. You are being silly. You are beautiful, inside and out. You are down to earth and real, and I like that about you. You have no reason to be scared," he explains.

He asks me once more at the end of the conversation, and I again express hesitation. I'm still scared, but I'm also feeling guilty because all of this is going on behind Linda's back. I guess I have not told her, because I'm afraid she'll ask me to stop communicating with him, and I'm not quite ready for this to end. Yet, I can't move forward either. I'm paralyzed with indecision.

Something that *should* bother me doesn't. His age. He's forty-two and I'm nineteen. I got past that a long time ago. He is smoking hot.

My indecision costs me. Not long after, Sly leaves for New Jersey to film a new movie called *Lockup*. He will be on location for three months.

CHAPTER SEVEN
Chocolate Covered Raisins

To my great excitement, Linda starts dating David Foster (the incredibly successful music producer, who works with huge music stars like Whitney Houston, Barbra Streisand and Michael Jackson), and it doesn't take long for the relationship to become serious. Again, I am impressed with Linda, and the men she draws. She only seems to get serious with people who are "the best" at what they do. I am again somewhat star-struck. As a piano player, I'm very familiar with the name David Foster. Many of the "hits" I used to play on the piano in my living room growing up (like "You're the Inspiration" and "Hard to Say I'm Sorry" by Chicago and the theme from the movie, *St. Elmo's Fire*) were produced by David.

Between David, Bruce, and Linda, we go out to eat often, because I don't know how to cook and Linda doesn't cook much either. She does make amazing Monster cookies, though, loaded with M&Ms, chocolate chips, and butterscotch chips. This year she also made a full course Turkey dinner, including a delicious pumpkin bisque. Maybe I can get her to teach me a thing or two.

When I do cook, my meals are simple. It's not actually what you'd call "cooking," so much as heating up. I make hamburger helper, mac and cheese, and hot dogs. Simple, basic, easy meals. I make dinner for the boys if we're not going out to eat, and they often pick at their plates, and don't eat much.

I'm not sure if it is the isolation, the boredom, the fact that I am surrounded by "perfect" bodies (including beautiful and thin Linda), or the unlimited supply of treats in the kitchen, but I think I am developing an eating disorder.

Growing up in the Midwest, I ate three square meals a day. Breakfast, dinner and supper, which often consisted of meat and potatoes. I was an active kid, always involved in sports and running around a lot, so I burned the calories right off. Throughout high school, and my first year of college in Rapid City, I continued to eat three big meals.

Now, I eat my own dinner, and then — because I come from a family where you clean your plate every night because "don't you know that kids are starving in Africa" — I finish what the boys have left on their plates too. I end up eating much more than a normal sized dinner portion.

A huge container of chocolate covered raisins always sat on the countertop in the kitchen, and every time I pass by it, I grab just a handful. Those "just-a-handfuls" add up to a "whole-lotta" chocolate by the end of the day. As if that isn't enough, there is the ice cream in the freezer calling my name. Linda's one treat to herself is Haagen Daaz Coffee and Swiss Almond flavored ice cream, which I absolutely love. I sneak bites of that all the time. A small bite here, a small bite there, and I find myself buying extra ice cream to restock what I have eaten so Linda won't know I am binging on her ice cream. Although she has probably already figured it out. I've noticeably gained weight. Then I feel so guilty and bad about myself that I starve myself for days. The boredom and loneliness continue, and eventually I get hungry, so I end up binging again.

I'm insecure about my body. I suppose it has something to do with being around all of the beautiful people in Malibu. There are so many thin, gorgeous women. Young teens to soccer moms — they all look stunning. I can't compete with them.

I try really hard not to eat. I starve myself because it's the quickest way to lose weight, and I tell myself that I will never again eat any bad or fattening foods like chocolate and ice cream. Which never works, of course, and after a few days of "being good," I end up binging on the forbidden items again. I feel so much guilt and shame. I cry at night when I'm going to sleep, promising myself that I'll do better tomorrow.

I feel lonely and sad, and I'm not quite sure why. When I moved to California and started working as a nanny, I stopped going to church. It wasn't an intentional rebellion. I work most Sundays, and on the rare day I have off, I am so exhausted and happy to have some free time, that church is not a priority on my to do list.

I guess I just don't think about God much. It doesn't ever cross my mind. On Sundays, I feel a bit of guilt, and think, I really should be in church, but that is about the extent of it. I pray occasionally, usually when I am facing something really tough with the boys. Then I pray and ask God to help me out. That is the extent of my current "relationship" with God.

I see him as a huge entity that sits on a throne in the sky, judges my actions, and answers my prayers only if I have been a good girl (or if I pray hard for a really long time). Despite my best intentions, I never seem to be good enough, and my prayers feel inadequate.

So I drift through my days. To rid myself of the unwanted pounds I have accumulated and assuage my guilt (about everything...it seems to be a prevailing theme in my life), I start running at the beach every day after dropping the kids at school. To get to the beach, I have to cross under a bridge, which happens to be the squatting grounds of several homeless men.

After a few days of seeing me pass by, one of them asks me, "Do you come here every day?"

"Yes, I sure do!" I say cheerfully.

I continue to run there every day, and I see those men there often. They are always quite friendly, and I greet them warmly. Am I so lonely, I ask myself one day, I count a group of homeless men among my friends?

At the end of the year, I fly back home to Minnesota for a much needed ten-day vacation to spend the holidays with my family. Sara is heading home for Christmas as well, and we are able to catch the same flight. As I land in the Fargo, North Dakota airport (which is actually closer to my home town than the Minneapolis airport), the vast difference between the world I had come from and the world I now live in slaps me in the face. Men in overalls (with big work boots covered in mud) walk by, their wives sporting festive Christmas sweaters. I love seeing "my people" again. They are my family, my friends, my roots, my culture — this is who I am. I'm not a Hollywood gal. It is a welcome relief and break from the image-conscious, affluent lifestyle I see around me in Malibu.

I realize I've been sucked into a new way of thinking, evaluating myself and my worth through how I look and what I have. I'm thankful to be back in the Midwest with family and friends who only care about what is on the inside. I realize that I miss the simplicity of life back home. In Los Angeles, life is so busy. The city is huge, and there is traffic everywhere you go. I feel an underlying stress trying to keep up with it all. The one huge plus about Southern California is the weather, but I have to admit I even miss the seasons. Maybe not winter so much, but definitely the colors and crispness of autumn, and I'm going to miss the fragrant blooms and sense of new beginnings in the spring. I have mixed feelings, torn between two homes pulling at my heart. I try to relax and enjoy being nurtured and taken care of by my mom. I appreciate the break from parenting the boys.

I recall Linda asking me a few weeks ago, "How could you move back to Minnesota after living here?"

I didn't say this to her, because I didn't want to put down the lifestyle that she loved so much, but I thought to myself, it has been a lot of fun and I've had opportunities that I never imagined and met superstar celebrities, but yes I could leave. I miss the simple life of home, down to earth people, nosy neighbors who know your business and actually worry about you if you don't follow your usual routine. I miss all of it, and yes, I can see myself moving back to the Midwest someday.

My family really wants me to come home. They are concerned, because I initially planned to take only the summer off from college, but now it has turned into a year. They want me to finish my college degree, and are concerned I am getting sidetracked. They know school has never been a priority for me.

They regularly tell me, "Pam, you *are* going back to school."

Followed by, "What about your dream to be a flight attendant? Do you still plan to pursue that?"

I know in my heart I will return to school. When I commit to something, I follow through. I am loyal and faithful, even to people I shouldn't be. I promise my parents that I will get my degree, and I will.

But, I don't want to pass up this once in a lifetime opportunity with Bruce and Linda. Something inside me tells me that I'm not done with my adventure in Los Angeles. I still retain my wanderlust, and hold on to my dream of traveling the world and exploring, but I'm not ready to leave Linda and the boys just yet. They are depending on me. And, I love them.

After a restful and rejuvenating visit with my family, I begin a new year at the Jenner home. When I walk in the door at Linda's house, the boys jump into my arms and smother me with hugs and kisses. I realize I love these boys more than ever. I really missed them when I was gone, and they obviously missed me. The questions, concerns, and frustrations slip to the back of my mind for the time being, and I dive back into my job.

Soon after I return to the Jenners, Sylvester Stallone begins to call me every day. He knows I am home by myself at Linda's house most days, and he is on location, away from his regular social life, and maybe a bit lonely. With Sly thousands of miles away in New Jersey, it seems safer to talk with him. We share stories of our families, childhoods, and previous relationships.

I confide in him about my first boyfriend, a "bad boy" whom I was forbidden by my parents to date. Unfortunately, they didn't explain or communicate exactly why I shouldn't see him or what they feared might happen. So I only heard "no," and chose to rebel against that authority. I made up stories, and snuck out to see him whenever I could. We were together at school and school activities (if my parents weren't around). It was a classic Romeo and Juliet tale, and I romanticized the forbidden love. My first experience with sex was at age sixteen when I was date raped. My plan up until then was to save myself for marriage, but that ruined everything. I was so hurt, and couldn't understand how someone who claimed to love me could treat me like that. It affected my belief in men, relationships, and true love. And probably God too. I think I blamed him, because he didn't prevent that from happening. Turns out my parents were right about the bad boy.

Sly tells me he is sorry for what I've been through, but reminds me that not all men are like that, and not to judge others based on the actions of one. He says he understands now why I've been so hesitant and afraid. I guess I understand more too.

As the days turn into weeks, our friendship blossoms, and he becomes my closest friend. He admits he was trying to make Linda jealous initially, but declares he is now truly interested in me. I conclude he couldn't be devoting this much time and energy just to make someone jealous, so I let my guard down, and choose to enjoy the friendship.

I confide in him about my eating disorder, and he is supportive and helpful. Every day, he questions me about my diet and exercise and holds me accountable. He continues to promise that we are going on a date when he returns to Los Angeles. With his support, I stop the starving and binging cycle, and begin to lose some weight. Having a friend to talk to helps my loneliness, and the possibility of dating Sly is a motivating factor to help me slim down.

Linda and David have gotten so serious that he moves into her house. Money was not an issue before, but with David in Linda's life, the family is catapulted into the stratosphere of the extremely wealthy, and it becomes commonplace for stars to drop by the house.

I realize quickly a wide chasm exists between celebrities whose fame has gone to their head versus those who maintain their down to earth attitude, and treat everyone, including the hired help, with dignity and respect. I wonder to myself what makes the difference. I reckon it has something to do with how they are raised and their core values.

On the down to earth end of the spectrum is Alan Thicke (the television star of *Growing Pains*), who is so nice and friendly. He came over for Thanksgiving last fall, and as I was busy in the kitchen, he stood there chatting with me for the longest time keeping me company.

Deidre Hall, star of the soap opera *Days of Our Lives* (which I had watched since I was a small child), comes over for lunch with Linda one day. I feel like I know her, and I want to sit down and have lunch with her too. She is as warm and friendly as the character she portrays on television.

Wayne Gretsky, who is a star player on the Los Angeles Kings hockey team, and his wife Janet Jones, a former actress, are close friends with David and Linda, so they start coming over quite often. They are both friendly and talkative with me.

Then there are those celebrities who don't say one word to me or even acknowledge my presence, but treat me like the hired help. I wonder about their parents. Where did they grow up? How were they treated? Stars are just people, some nice and others not so nice. I make a decision. I will no longer be awestruck when I see a celebrity, but rather wait to see how they treat others (or me) before I decide whether to be impressed with them.

I enjoyed my trips to Tahoe last fall with Bruce and the boys, so I'm excited when we head up again in January. Lake Tahoe is beautiful and picturesque covered in a layer of white snow, like a winter wonderland. My very first day of skiing is quite an experience. I spend the entire day "snow-plowing" down the slopes, while Brandon and Brody, who are already expert skiers, swoosh by me, covering me with a dusting of snow.

The next morning, I am so sore I can barely get out of bed. It is not my nature to give up, but I am aching and frustrated from an entire day of failure that I don't want to face it again. I hear a knock on my door, hobble over to answer it, and there is Bruce, ready to hit the slopes.

"Please, Bruce, let me stay at the cabin. I can't go out today. I am so sore. I can't move," I beg.

"Pam, you *are* going." I can tell by the look on his face that he will not take no for an answer, so I give in, take a few pain relievers, and get myself dressed.

As I start to move around, and the pain reliever kicks in, I begin to feel much better. While I take the ski lift to the top of a beginner slope, Bruce stands at the bottom, watching to see how much I have learned. He spent many hours the previous day teaching me how to ski, but I realize as I'm flying down the slope that he neglected to show me how to stop. I do fairly well skiing down the hill, but wipe out the entire line of people who are waiting to get on the ski lift. Lying on the ground, with my skis splayed out in different directions, snow in my face and hair, I look up at Bruce.

He shakes his head sarcastically. "Nice job, Pam."

All I can do is laugh, partly from humiliation, but also because the scene is like something from a movie. How do I get myself into these situations?

Every morning, we go out to breakfast at a restaurant called Post Office. I feel proud and special walking next to Bruce, as heads turn and people whisper, as they try to figure out, "Is that Bruce Jenner?" and "Who is that girl with him?"

My relationship with the boys has changed so drastically from those first few weeks when we were all adjusting to each other. Yet, as I'm sure most young boys do, they test me at times, and it can be challenging.

In February, the boys and I meet a friend of mine from Minnesota for lunch in Beverly Hills. The boys are angels during lunch, but on the ride home they are misbehaving. I ask them numerous times to quiet down and stop pestering each other, yet the noise level in the car continues to rise, until they are screaming at each other.

I am frustrated and having a hard time concentrating on driving. I finally pull over to the side of the rode to discipline them.

"Brandon and Brody, I've had enough," I tell them firmly. "I've asked you three times to stop calling each other names. Hand me your cars."

They are both playing with toy cars I had bought earlier. I take the cars out of their hands. Brody is very upset.

"I wish you were fired," he yells.

I am so frustrated with both of them and their behavior, and now Brody has thrown a dagger that hurts. I begin to cry.

They both look at me with surprise. Brandon reaches over and hits Brody.

"Why did you say that to her?" he asks.

"I'm sorry, Pam," Brody offers. "I didn't mean it."

I wipe my tears without saying anything, turn around, and drive off. The car is quiet for the twenty minutes it takes us to get home. That dagger hurt. More than the little boy who hurled it could ever know. That's my greatest fear. I'm not his mom. There are no assurances. I love him. I love his brother. Yet, I could be gone tomorrow. By my choice or theirs. It's a strange place to navigate — a tenuous existence with no assurances. Yet, how can I give anything but my all? I care for them; I protect them; and I love them.

When we arrive home and get out of the car, the boys run over to me and give me kisses and hugs. All is forgiven.

That night, as I'm lying in bed thinking about the day, I hear the door open and see a small form in the shadows. Brandon crawls into bed with me. I hug and kiss him, and cuddle him close. He sleeps with me all night. I think he's making sure I don't go anywhere. I love them like they are my own.

As much as I love being a nanny, it is not what I plan to do for the rest of my life. I love playing with Brandon and Brody, nurturing them, and acting like a kid myself. And I'm so thankful for the incredible opportunities

I've had to meet interesting people. However, it is challenging being a live-in nanny. I am never really "off the clock." The lines between *my* life and *their* life seem a hazy gray.

I reflect back on my conversations with my parents over the holidays and realize I need to get serious about school again. The biggest decision I have to make is whether to go back to Rapid City or stay in California.

One day, Bruce suggests, "Why don't you go to Pepperdine? It's right up the street."

"There's no way I can afford Pepperdine, Bruce."

"Then apply for a scholarship. You are obviously very musical. You could get one," he encourages.

I miss my family back home, and have begun to realize I even miss the simple life of the Midwest. But I love Linda and the boys, and there's still the unknown possibility of what might happen with Sly. I'm torn, and a clear decision about my future eludes me.

February 28, 1989
Dear Mom,

Happy Birthday honey! I love you! I talked to my bro today. He was eating dinner (we call it lunch here in California). It sounds like he's getting excited for this quarter to get over with. I can't believe my big brother is almost done with college.

Thinking about school gives me a headache! I don't know what to do. I could go back to school in Rapid City. After all, I'm already enrolled and I'd be done in one year. Then again, there are some great schools here in California that I could go to for practically free, live in the guest house and babysit evenings. Anyways, I've just been applying everywhere. Who knows, I may not even be accepted to them all so that would narrow down my choices.

What do you think I should do? I went to Pepperdine University today to pick up an application and check out the campus. Pepperdine is about two miles from here and they have a great music program. All I did all afternoon is fill out the application.

I was supposed to go out with a friend tonight, but it's 9:23pm and I haven't heard from her. I guess I get pretty bummed when that happens because then I'm stuck here with nothing to do and nowhere to go. I can't really take the car either. On my days off, if I stick around the house, it's not even like a day off.

Brandon and Brody are the loves of my life. They keep my chin up and a smile on my face. They're excited to meet "Nanny Pam's" mom and dad. Mom, you have a great birthday! I wish I could be with you to give you a great big hug and kiss, and to tell you how much I love you!

Pam

The boys and Bruce have taken to calling me Nanny Pam. Bruce has three Pam's in his life. He has a sister named Pam, a secretary named Pam, and of course, me. So he starts to refer to me as Nanny Pam to differentiate. Whenever he says that, I remind him, "No, I'm the *best* Pam!"

After visiting Pepperdine, I am more excited about staying in California. The campus is beautiful with a huge green lawn that overlooks the ocean. Students sit in groups talking while others take naps in the sun. It seems peaceful, idyllic and it is so close by. Pepperdine is also a Christian college, which I think my parents will like.

I talk to Linda about my desire to go back to college and present the idea of working part-time. Brandon and Brody are a bit older now, and are in school most of the time anyway. I'm so happy when she says she is very agreeable to that arrangement.

I turn in my application to Pepperdine, and apply for scholarships as well. I tell myself that the decision about whether to stay or go will depend on whether I get a scholarship. If I get one, I stay and attend Pepperdine. If I don't get a scholarship, I will head back to Rapid City this summer and go back to school there.

One day in March, Bruce drives the boys and me to Ojai, which is northeast of Los Angeles. As I ride in the front seat of his white Thunderbird Super Coupe, the sunroof is open, the windows are down, and the wind is blowing through our hair. We have the music cranked and it is a beautiful summer day. A Madonna song comes on the radio. "Like a Prayer" — it is the first time I've ever heard it. I feel alive, and free, and so thankful for all the adventures I've already had since moving to California.

Bruce never fails to surprise me. One day, as we are talking, I notice that Bruce is looking at me funny.

"What?" I ask as he stares at my face.

"You should probably have a little taken off your nose."

Huh? I'm nineteen. It has *never* occurred to me that I might need a nose job, despite the fact that the Behan family is known for their "ski-slope" noses.

I look at him like he is crazy and say, "Yeah, well I don't think I will be doing that any time soon."

I guess in the land of the beautiful and perfect people, there is always some "work" that can be done.

CHAPTER EIGHT
Three Dates with Rocky

Filming of his movie wraps in early April, and Sly calls me the day he arrives back to his home in Beverly Hills.

"Pam, I want you to meet me at the beach house tomorrow." (He has a second home in Malibu.) "If you are not there I will come by and pick you up. I mean it."

"I'm not sure," I say, nervous and terrified, yet excited and thrilled to see him again. "I'll think about it. Maybe. I'll see if I can get away."

The next day, as lady luck graciously obliges, Linda is not home. The boys are at school, so I have a few hours during which I can get away unnoticed. I am indecisive — should I go or not? For hours, I wrestle with my thoughts. I feel guilt about Linda, since she has no clue we have been talking all of these months. I am still scared and nervous about dating a big star. Ultimately, the pull of my attraction for Sly is too strong.

I don't leave a note or tell the maid where I am going. I jump in the station wagon, embarrassed that I'll be pulling up to Sly's Malibu mansion in such a dilapidated car.

I arrive at his Malibu home, which sits right on the beach. It is painted a shade of pinkish-peach (a fact that surprises me, given his manly action star status). When

I knock, a man (not sure if he is a butler, assistant or friend) answers the door and lets me in. I give him my name and tell him Sly is expecting me. As he ushers me through the foyer, I glance around the house. The living room ahead has floor to ceiling windows, offering incredible views of the ocean just below. The man gives me a glass of water and seats me at the table in the kitchen to wait for Sly, who hasn't arrived yet from his home in Beverly Hills.

I am anxious, nervous, and scared, but full of expectation and excitement. The refrigerator has a black glass door, and I see the reflection of Sly as he walks in behind me. The look on his face makes me instantly relax — he is genuinely happy to see me.

Ours eyes meet and he says, "I really thought I'd have to come and get you."

I stand up, turn around, and he embraces me in a tight, long hug.

"See, we fit together perfectly," he murmurs into my hair. He is not much taller than me. We look each other straight in the eye.

He leads me around his house. There are many pictures of him in his movie roles. The most impressive room in his house, in my opinion, is the walk in closet. I've never seen anything like that before. It is huge — twice the size of the bedroom I now live in at Linda's. As we stand there in the closet, I notice he is wearing a necklace with a small pendant that has the inscription "DTA."

I ask him, "What does DTA mean?"

"Don't trust anyone," he responds.

That's sad and depressing, I think. "Why do you feel that way?"

"Just wait twenty years," he explains, "and you'll feel that way too." He tells me that people always seem to take advantage of him.

As we talk, I notice he has a football jersey with "Stallone" written on the back hanging in his closet.

He must see me looking longingly at the jersey, because he asks, "Do you want anything?"

I say no, because I don't want to be like everyone else.

He glances at me, surprise in his eyes. He takes a step towards me and kisses me gently. It is a good kiss, and I want it to last forever. But I can't relax, appreciate it, or fully enjoy it because I am completely overwhelmed that I am actually kissing Sylvester Stallone, the superstar I have been obsessed with for so many years. It's as if I'm kissing not only a man, but an icon, a hero, an impossible dream come true — the culmination of

years of infatuation and fantasies. It is too much. It is overwhelming. Because it is "forbidden fruit," it only makes the feelings more intense.

I am floating, as he steps back and looks at me. I gaze back at him, saying nothing, and he takes me by the hand and leads me around his house, showing me more pictures, memorabilia, talking about people who are important to him.

Questions form. What does this mean? What is going to happen? How serious is he about me? Was it all about the challenge, and will he lose interest now that he's got me?

His low voice is mesmerizing, lilting, carrying me off into this reverie that has now become reality. I drift, hover and soar, until our time together must end, as I rush to pick up Brandon and Brody from school.

He protests, asking me to stay, so he can take me out for dinner on a proper date. I decline. I don't want Linda to find out and fire me.

He tries again, "Don't you think you could find another job? I could find you a job anywhere."

But I like working for Linda, and I don't want another job. Given how she reacted when I told her Sly had called to talk to me last fall, I figure she won't be happy if she finds out I am dating him. No nights out on the town, no extravagant dates, no wining and dining for me; this will have to be a covert affair.

I leave on cloud nine and float there for the next few days.

Later that week, Sly invites me to his Beverly Hills house. I spend hours getting ready, discarding one outfit after another, as I try to find the perfect attire. The first date felt like a dream, almost like it didn't happen. I am looking forward to a second date, so I can actually be more present, and absorb and remember what he says to me.

My emotions are in turmoil, because I'm caught in the middle. I so badly want to tell Linda what is going on, but I'm worried she will fire me. I love Linda and the boys, and I look forward to the trips to Tennessee and Canada that are coming up. But, I don't want to pass up this opportunity to date a man I have been obsessed with for years. After many sleepless nights and tortured days, I choose adventure and the possibility of love.

Sly gives me directions to his Beverly Hills home, and I try to follow them, but end up getting lost. I don't plan adequately for traffic either. I end up arriving more than an hour late, so I am stressed and nervous. He is planning on attending an event later in the evening, so our time is limited.

I drive up the long, twisting driveway with thick foliage on either side. It is definitely a mansion, and what I would expect from a star of his magnitude. I reach a huge security gate, which has one entrance for arriving cars, and a second gate for cars that are leaving. I stop and touch the intercom button, which is answered by a male voice that instructs me to come in. The huge gate buzzes and slowly begins to open. Just like you see in the movies, I think.

I park my nanny-mobile, which looks sorely out of place next to the exotic cars parked on the cobblestone in front of the mansion. What is a girl from Norcross doing here?

As I get out of the car, I look towards the front door, and there is Sly waiting for me, looking stunning in a three-piece suit. I am suddenly breathless, held captive by the spell of my attraction to this man.

He gathers me into his arms for a long hug and then holds me back so he can look at me.

"Hi," he says simply in *that* voice, which unravels me.

He plants a tender kiss on my lips, grabs my hand, and leads me into his home.

As he did in Malibu, Sly guides me around his house, which is luxurious and opulent to me, filled with beautiful furnishings, works of art, and more memorabilia and pictures from his many films. He explains the memorabilia, shows me photos, and recounts stories from his days on the sets of his movies. It is all very interesting, but he might be talking about taxes and accounting, and I'd be just as enthralled. His voice mesmerizes me.

Despite my hope to be more present, I am again drawn into a state of otherworldliness, a sense that I am floating above myself, watching the events unfold. Being with Sly feels surreal, and the thought keeps returning, what am *I* doing here?

The evening ends too soon, as Sly must rush off to the event at which his presence is required. His kiss still lingers on my lips, as I retreat through the security gate, glancing in my rear view mirror as the huge gate slowly closes on a world I know isn't mine to hold. The visit was so brief, almost fleeting, as if a snippet of a dream I'm not quite sure I had. I sense it is destined to be just that — a few passing moments to cherish and remember.

April 20, 1989
Dear Dad and Mom,

Hi there! I went to see Sly at his Beverly Hills house on Monday.
We had fun. He had some dinner to go to at 6:30, but I got stuck in
traffic and lost, so I didn't get there until 6. He felt sorry for me
and didn't leave til 8. I also baked him some cookies. He loved them!
I have pictures of us. I love it!

I love you too,
Pam

When I am with Sly, his presence is overwhelming for me, yet when we talk on the phone, we are just two people that enjoy each other's company. He is simply a friend who happens to be really famous. During the three months he was in New Jersey, we spent an incredible amount of time on the phone and talked about every topic imaginable. I wish I could feel that comfortable when I am with him on a date.

I don't have much free time in my schedule, and it is hard to plan time together with Sly when I'm sneaking around behind Linda's back to date him. About a week later, Sly invites me to see him again at the beach house in Malibu. I only have a couple hours, since I can't explain my absence to Linda, but thankfully, this time I am not so overwhelmed with him. I am able to enjoy my time with a man named Sly, and forget, for a while anyway, his superstar status.

I arrive home to find a letter from Pepperdine University laying on my bed. I rush over, grab it, and tear it open, fingers trembling. I have been accepted as a student for the fall semester of 1989, and I have received a half scholarship to study music. I am thrilled. I was hoping for a full scholarship, but it's enough to make it feasible. I realize I will have to find a second job to come up with the difference, which amounts to about $10,000 per year. I decide I will worry about that later, as we are heading out of town.

A few days later, Linda, Brandon, Brody, and I fly to Nashville. Linda is on the cast of *Hee Haw* (a country-themed television show), and they film her scenes for the season all at once, during a month-long stay. So while Linda is filming during the day, the boys and I explore Nashville. It is actually a really fun vacation, unlike any I'd had as a child. We all stay in a nice hotel, and the boys and I go to the Opryland amusement park every single day. We get to eat *every* meal — breakfast, lunch and dinner — at a restaurant.

June 15, 1989
Dear Dad & Mom,

Hello father! Hello mother! This is your daughter. How are you doing? Great, I hope!

We're having fun here. The kids have been good, for the most part, except yesterday at Opryland (a big amusement park). It started to rain so I got the kids under a sheltered area and bought them some grape drinks. Well, they got bored and decided to have a grape juice fight with all of their new clothes on. I got mad and said, "We're leaving as soon as the rain stops." Brody didn't wait. He just took off running, without a clue where he was going, through the park. I started to run after him and he ran faster. Let's just say that when I caught him, he was in BIG TROUBLE. Anyway, I lived through it and here I am telling it.

The boys and I have been going to Opryland almost every day because they have free passes. It's fun but the rides are getting old. It's better than sitting around the hotel or studio every day though. Brody is scared of most of the rides but the other day Brandon and I tricked him into going on this one water ride. We told him the hill wasn't steep at all, but it actually was. Anyway, after he went on it, he really loved it and wanted to go on it again and again. We knew he'd love it! Gotta hit the hay.

I love you,
Pam

On weekends we drive to the home in Memphis that Elvis bought for Linda's father, "Papa." I enjoy exploring Memphis with Linda, the boys and her family. We attend Memphis in May (a huge music festival held on the banks of the Mississippi), and eat dinner on Beale Street. Elvis used to perform in some of these restaurants, so it is fun being here with his former girlfriend. Some of the restaurants serve "Elvis Favorites" like fried pickles on a stick and peanut butter and banana sandwiches.

I am busy with the boys from morning to night. And I don't want any long distance phone calls to Sly showing up on Linda's hotel bill, so it is hard to stay in touch. We talk briefly when I have a few moments to call him from a pay phone.

One weekend at Papa's house, I put a birthday card addressed to Sly in the mailbox, trying to time it — right before the mailman comes — so Linda won't see it.

Later that evening, the house is filled with Linda's family, including her brother and his family, Papa, Brandon and Brody, David Foster, and me. We are all sitting around after dinner chatting. At one point, there is a lull in the conversation, and Linda clears her throat.

"Pam, I noticed that you put a card in the mailbox to Sylvester Stallone," Linda says sweetly in her Southern drawl. "Do you even know him?"

"Oh yes, he *knows* me," I retort, looking directly at her, and hold her gaze until she looks away.

I understand why she needed to ask me, but I am surprised at how she chose to do it. I wish she had asked me privately instead of in front of the entire family, which was so embarrassing.

It is the event that seals the fate of my relationship with Sly. I realize I don't want to lose Linda and the boys. I followed my heart and had a good adventure, but deep down, I know that there is no future along that path, only eventual heartbreak. It sure did wonders for my self-esteem, though, and for that I will always be thankful to Sly. He was a true friend to me and treated me with kindness and respect.

Linda is hurt, but after avoiding the issue for a few days, we finally discuss it, and I apologize for going behind her back. Thankfully, she forgives me. She seems to understand how hard it was for me to avoid his magnetic pull.

I stop calling Sly, and since he has no way of reaching me, the relationship fizzles. He calls once or twice after we return from Tennessee, but the heat has gone out of the relationship. We don't discuss it or officially end it, as there was nothing official about "us" other than a friendship. My dream of being Mrs. Sylvester Stallone came so close to becoming reality. Not really, but it was a grand adventure.

CHAPTER NINE
Work or Vacation?

I am so busy this summer; I don't have much time to feel sad about the breakup with Sly. David's presence in our lives brings many new activities. He has three children from his previous relationship. Sara is eight, Erin is six, and Jordan is two. They haven't spent much time at the house with us yet, but David will have them for summer vacation.

My parents drive out from Minnesota to visit me. I am thrilled to see them, show them around, and connect my two worlds. Linda has graciously invited them to stay in the guesthouse. My parents are quite impressed with everything, and Linda and David are so friendly and polite. I'm secretly relieved, because I know they've harbored many doubts about my decision to stay in California.

We tour the campus at Pepperdine, spend a day at Disneyland, and go out to eat a few times in Malibu. David invites my parents to his studio, and we get to meet Celine Dion, a Canadian singer. David is producing her first English album. She

Celine, David, Mom, and Dad

73

chats with us, takes a picture with my mom and dad, and is so sweet, kind, and friendly.

One night, I decide to take them out for a special dinner at a fancy place. I think it will be a nice memory for them. I choose a ritzy and expensive restaurant on the beach in Malibu called Splash that not many people even know about. It is hidden, exclusive, and honestly I really can't afford it. But I don't care. I want to treat my mom and dad (and myself) to a once in a lifetime night out. We order a bottle of wine, appetizers, fresh seafood, *and* dessert. The service is impeccable and the food mouth-watering. I am beginning to feel a bit nervous, as I have done some figures in my head, and I'm afraid the tab is going to be huge. I am hoping and praying that I brought enough cash with me. It will be embarrassing to have to ask my parents to chip in some cash. I wait for the bill, but when the waiter returns to fill our water glasses with no bill, I inquire.

"Excuse me, sir, can we get our bill?" I ask politely.

"Oh I'm sorry, Miss, I thought you already knew. Your bill has been paid."

"What?" I exclaim, in shock. "By whom?"

"I'm not sure, Miss, but I can find out."

He returns shortly and tells me that our dinner was paid for by David Foster. I immediately tear up, and my mom does too. It is one of the nicest things anyone has ever done for me.

It is hard to say good-bye when my parents leave, but I'm thankful they finally got to see my life here, and I feel like they are softer in their tone and manner towards me. They understand my decision. They seemed to really like Pepperdine, and I'm thankful they got to see the campus before school starts.

Linda has agreed to let me move into the guesthouse when school starts in the fall, so I will have more privacy. She will hire a new nanny to move into my room in the main house. The boys will have a new, full-time nanny Monday through Friday, and I will help out on the weekends. In exchange, I get to stay in the guesthouse rent-free.

I remember one of my classmates from high school was interested in being a nanny. I give her a call, and she is very excited about the possibility. After a phone interview with Linda a few days later, Julie is offered the job and makes plans to arrive in Malibu at the end of August.

The guesthouse takes care of my room and board, but there's still that $10,000 annual tuition I need to pay. It is time to look for a second job. Sly has told me numerous times that he can get me a job anywhere. One of the placcs he mentions is Gladstones, a local eatery on the beach in Malibu. I drive over to the restaurant and fill out an application for a hostess position, and write Sylvester Stallone as a reference on my application, along with David Foster, Bruce Jenner, and Linda Jenner. Name-dropping actually works. I get the job and will start at the end of August when we return from vacation.

David owns a fifty-three foot yacht, which we are taking to British Columbia (he grew up in Canada) for a month. I am so excited, and I can hardly wait for the end of July (when we are scheduled to leave). I spent many summers fishing and camping in Canada with my family, so I am thrilled I get to go along. I know I will be working the entire time, taking care of Brandon and Brody, as well as David's three girls, but I don't mind. It will be an amazing adventure.

After weeks of preparation, the much-anticipated trip finally arrives. With three adults, five children, and an insane amount of luggage, we board a flight at the Los Angeles airport and fly to Vancouver. The five kids are my responsibility on the airplane, and I focus much of my energy on keeping little Jordan occupied, making funny faces and telling her stories.

David keeps his yacht in Victoria (where he grew up) on Vancouver Island (which is across the bay from Vancouver) year round, and employs a man named Max to maintain it. We take a ferry from Vancouver to get to the yacht in Victoria. It is a beautiful and quaint city right on the bay. Cobblestone streets are lined with old-fashioned streetlights and hanging flowerpots. It is one of the loveliest places I've ever been. Quaint shops and restaurants line the busy streets, which are filled with people in their summer attire. Everyone looks happy. It reminds me of my recent trip to Disneyland with my parents. Maybe Victoria is the second happiest place on earth.

As we board the yacht, I feel like a princess. I've only seen "boats" like this in the movies, and I never thought I'd ever set foot on one, much less spend an entire month cruising around the coast of Canada. It makes me think of a movie that came out a few years ago called *Overboard* with Goldie Hawn. She plays a wealthy socialite who takes a cruise on a huge yacht. (She ends up getting kidnapped by a bachelor and his three rambunctious boys and is forced to be their maid and cook. That part of the story I don't relate to, thank God.) It feels surreal being on this huge yacht, and I think I must be the luckiest girl in the world.

The yacht has two bedrooms, plus quarters for Max (who comes along with us to drive and care for the boat), a surprisingly large kitchen, and good size living room. I assume that David and Linda will take the large bedroom, and soon learn that the girls share the second bedroom, the boys sleep in the living room on the large comfy couches, and the kitchen table folds into a bed, which is where I will sleep.

The front deck is quite spacious, with many places to sit on brightly colored cushions. There is plenty of open space for the kids to play, and the yacht is stocked with jet skis, rafts, fishing gear, and other toys, so it's a kid paradise.

Once we are out in the ocean, I am again overwhelmed. The view of the coastline, the ocean, and the endless blue sky with fluffy white clouds is breathtaking and indescribable, like a picture perfect postcard. On the second day in the ocean, a pod of orca whales swim near the yacht. They are so close we can see their eyes and teeth. I think of the Jacques Cousteau movies I used to watch in high school social studies class with Mr. Magnuson (not sure how Jacques Cousteau related to Social Studies, but we loved the movies), and feel like I am on my own marine expedition. The kids scream with excitement, which actually makes the whales follow us and speak to us with their plaintive, wailing call. With the sun on my face, the wind in my hair, and the spray of salty seawater on my lips, I take a picture in my heart, knowing this is an experience I *never* want to forget.

The days pass quickly, as we are busy from morning to night. On the days we are hanging out on the yacht, David or Max take the kids jet skiing; we fish off the back; I play cards and board games with the kids; or we all hang out on the deck. Brody is in heaven out here in the beauty of nature, and he loves fishing, which we try to do every day. Every few days, we dock at another port — each town is quaint, unique, and beautiful. Often, we go out for dinner at a local restaurant, and sometimes spend the night in a cottage or lodge. David and Linda pay my way for everything. I could have come on this vacation without a cent and been just fine.

The older kids, Brandon, Sara, and Erin, are relatively independent, so I mainly keep an eye on Brody and little Jordan. David is a hands-on dad with his girls, and of course, Linda dotes on her boys, so I have a lot of help. It is a group effort.

Several times during the month, we head back to Victoria, where David's mom and sister Jeannie live, and spend several nights with them. I develop a huge crush on Jeannie's son, Lane, who is in his early twenties, home from college for the summer, and hot. We are in the backyard one afternoon, and I am flirting with him, hoping to catch his attention. Trying to position myself close to Lane, I sit down on a plastic bench that looks like it's meant to hold flowerpots, not people. I make an impression all right, when the bench brakes, and I end up on my bottom with a scraped, bleeding leg, and a sheepish grin.

David has a friend in Victoria named Charlie White, who owns a fishing boat. He takes David and the boys out fishing several times, and my little Brody has the biggest grin on his face when he returns. I thought my brother and I liked to fish, but our love for the sport pales in comparison to Brody. That child would spend every day of his life fishing if he could.

David and Linda tell me that Kevin Costner and his wife, Cindy, will be spending a day on the yacht with us. I can't wait to meet him. He is a huge movie star, but seems like he'd be a really nice guy.

David has been working on the soundtrack for a new movie coming out that Kevin is starring in and directing called *Dances with Wolves*. We are docked in one of the ports along the coast when Kevin and Cindy come aboard. David introduces me and tells Kevin that I am from Minnesota, and that I went to school in South Dakota, which is where *Dances with Wolves* was filmed.

Kevin is so warm and talkative and reminds me of a friendly neighbor. He sure doesn't act like a celebrity. When he hears that I spent time in South Dakota, he seems excited and starts chatting with me about how beautiful the area is. He calls South Dakota "a well kept secret." Kevin's parents actually live in Spearfish, SD, which is not far from Rapid City. Kevin even owns some casinos and restaurants in Deadwood, SD, a tourist attraction that resembles an old west mining town. I am surprised to find we have so much common ground to talk about.

As we laugh and chat, I realize the conversation is getting longer and longer. Linda and Cindy are sitting next to us on the deck of the yacht, saying a few words to each other here and there, but mostly just listening to Kevin and me talk. I vaguely notice the noise level in the background getting louder. The kids, who are my responsibility, are running around the deck and screaming, but since I am enjoying talking to Kevin Costner, I'm really not paying much attention to them.

I glance at Linda, and she gives me a look that makes me realize it is time to go and tend to the kids.

"Kevin, it has been fun chatting, but I better get back to the kids now," I say regretfully, wishing I could continue the conversation.

Not only is he very nice, but I really miss the Midwest, and I am enjoying talking about "back home." It is definitely a moment when I wish I am a guest, and not just the nanny.

David has his keyboard along on the trip, and occasionally, he sits down to play or plunk out a new tune he's working on. Many nights, I have fallen asleep in my room back in Malibu, looking at the stars through my skylight, and listening to David play in the living room. Linda is an English major and has written poetry for years, so David has been encouraging Linda to  write lyrics. It doesn't surprise me that they are working on a song together on the boat. Linda has written some lyrics about a "grown-up Christmas list" and reads them out loud. David starts to tap out a few notes, and a beautiful melody appears. I love it immediately. Over the next few days they write the rest of the lyrics and finish the bones of the song. I wonder to myself if I will hear the song on the radio someday. I hope so, I think, because I will always remember this moment on the yacht surrounded by the beauty of the ocean and British Columbia.

The trip ends much too soon, and it's time to head back to Malibu, my heart full of memories of a dream vacation. I recognize how blessed I am to have enjoyed an incredible trip that few people in this world ever have the chance to experience.

August 13, 1989
Dear Dad, Mom & Bro,

Well hello everybody! It was really nice to talk to you this morning. I miss your voices. I'm in Vancouver right now on a layover in the airport. Besides having a cold, I've had a great time in Canada! It's beautiful here and David and Linda really were good to me. The boys were good too.

Julie flies in tomorrow night, so that doesn't give me too much time to unpack everybody's stuff and move into the guest house. This coming week is going to be busy for me. Julie (I call her Joe) will be here so I'll be helping her get adjusted, but I'll also have a lot to do of my own. I have to register for classes, maybe get some shots, start working at Gladstones and move into the guest house. Linda is paying me half of my pay for this week, which is fine with me.

I really love you all more than chocolate. (That's a lot!)
Pam

Now that college has started, my schedule is pretty crazy. I go to my classes during the day, work at Gladstones after school in the evening, and study late into the night. On the weekends when most college kids have fun with their friends, party, go to the beach and generally enjoy life, I am working.

To be honest, I don't mind it, because I finally have a social life. I make some dear friends at college and at Gladstones. I even start dating, which Bruce seems to find quite amusing. I'm not sure why. I think it's partly his personality — he's a jokester — and partly because of the relationship we have. He's like a big brother to me, and that's what big brothers do. They tease their little sisters.

A guy I met in my orientation class named Tony comes over to Linda's house one night to watch a movie. Bruce and his girlfriend, Jane (who he's been casually dating for a few months), are there. I am surprised how nervous I am. I almost feel like I'm bringing a date home to meet the parents.

Tony arrives, and Bruce introduces himself and Jane, and then interjects, "Wow, Pam, you finally got a date?"

"Bruce!" I exclaim, turning red, "Stop it!"

"It's been about two years now right?" he continues, with a huge grin on his face.

I hit him on the arm, but can't suppress a laugh. Tony is smiling but looks a little concerned.

"So what are we going to do tonight?" Bruce asks.

I didn't know he was planning to chaperone the evening. When I realize I'm not getting rid of him, I decide to embrace the unexpected double date. I had rented a video earlier in the day that is appropriate for the boys to watch too. Unfortunately, the VCR downstairs is broken, so we have to watch upstairs in the master bedroom.

I pop in the movie, and we all pile onto the king size bed. Bruce, Jane, Brandon, Brody, Tony, and me, with Louie snoring at the foot of the bed.

In October, I turn twenty-one. Linda surprises me with a professional massage treatment. I've never had a massage before, so it is quite a treat. The massage therapist arrives at the house, sets up her own little massage table in my bedroom, and I enjoy an hour of wonderful, luxurious, relaxation. My birthday falls on a Saturday, and despite my new friends and social life at school and Gladstones, I choose to spend this momentous birthday with my uncle in San Diego. Linda allows me to take the station wagon, and I drive down to share my first legal margarita with my fifty-year old uncle.

I rarely have time off, and when I do, I never dare ask to use Linda or David's car. They won't mind if I use the station wagon, but I won't be caught dead driving that car with my new friends. I either take the bus or a friend picks me up.

Julie, my school mate who took over as full-time nanny, quit and flew home after a few months. Linda then hired a new full-time nanny named Anne, who is fun and outgoing. I spent a week training her, and we got along quite well. So, we have begun to hang out together socially.

One Friday, Anne and I plan to go out to the Sage Brush Cantina in Woodland Hills, a popular night spot. David knows we are looking forward to it, and he offers to let me use his beautiful black Mercedes. I can't believe it!

We are so cool dressed in our hottest outfits, with extra makeup for dramatic effect. We pull up into the valet section, and I hand the keys over.

"Take good care of my baby," I say.

"Oh yes, Miss. Of course."

Wow, I could get used to this life, I think, as we enter the bar. In the back of my head, though, I remember that the clock will soon strike midnight, and my Cinderella fairytale will be over. I'll be back to driving the pumpkin. It is fun to pretend, if only for a night.

Another perk of working for David is that he owns season tickets to the Kings hockey games. One weekend, he can't make it to a game, and he invites me and his personal assistant, Keala Ona Ona Pua Hinano Barbie Jo Campton (her real name which takes me forever to memorize), to go to the game. The seats are right behind the goalie box, so we get to see all of the action at the goal. David also has passes to the Forum Club, so after the game, Keala and I hang out and try to meet all of the hockey players. I develop a huge crush on Luc Robitaille, and hope that David will have many conflicts develop in his schedule that will prevent him from going to other games.

CHAPTER TEN
Ponch and Goldie

I finally have a car, which has given me a newfound sense of freedom. It is a 1980 two-tone, blue Thunderbird. I feel like I have developed a life of my own. I'm not just "the nanny" anymore. I have friends from school and work, a car, a social life, and my own schedule. I realize I lost myself that first year of being a nanny. It is nice to have my own life, my own responsibilities and priorities.

On my first day of college, I meet my dear friend, Smitty. We have a class called convocation (chapel), which is required attendance for all students. Seating is assigned, and I happen to sit next to Smitty, who is on the tennis team. We hit it off, and she becomes my "go to girl" for fun times.

Our birthdays are only a few weeks apart in October, and Smitty buys us both rollerblades. She has rollerbladed before, but I am a novice. Since we consider ourselves quite athletic, we head up a fairly steep hill, thinking we'll get a great glute workout from the climb. I am doing fairly well at this new sport, and I am quite proud of myself. We turn around at the top and head down the sidewalk. I realize I forgot one fairly important point, which reminds me of an escapade on the ski slopes not too long ago.

"Smitty, oh my gosh! Smitty! I don't know how to stop! What do I do?" I scream.

"Grab onto the pole," she yells back, as she glides to a stop near the bottom.

As I quickly approach the bottom of the hill, I debate my options. I can either keep going and roll right off the edge of the sidewalk onto a busy street where I'll likely be run over and killed, *or* I can run smack into the concrete light pole at the bottom of the sidewalk. I choose the latter. I slam straight into the pole, wrapping my arms and legs around it. The horrendous pain is dulled faintly by the realization that I am *not* going to die.

Smitty is doubled over, laughing hysterically.

"I just peed my pants!" she exclaims, laughing even harder.

I crumple over, laughing until I cry, finally collapsing on the ground in a heap.

I am enjoying my part-time job at Gladstones. The restaurant is a famous hot spot for tourists and locals to hang out. It is right off PCH, literally on the beach, and a great place to find celebrities. Working in the California sunshine, in a tank top, a stone's throw away from the ocean is amazing. To make it even better, I make great money, usually about one hundred dollars each day for a five or six-hour shift. Being on my feet all day is tiring, but I still enjoy it, mostly because I finally have a social life. I get to hang out with my peers. Often a group of us go out after work for something to eat. Our favorite hangout is a Mexican restaurant called TexMex. They have the best chips and salsa, and good margaritas.

As hostess, it is my job to seat our guests. One day, I glance towards the front door and see Erik Estrada step into the restaurant. He was the star of *CHIPS*, one of my favorite television shows from the 1980s. I beg and plead to the head hostess to let me seat him. He must have seen me asking her, or maybe the gigantic smile on my face reveals the star struck girl beneath, because he flirts with me on the way to the table. I keep peeking at him as I resume my hostess duties. He is a fine looking man.

On a sunny afternoon a few months later, I am waiting tables (I've been promoted) on the patio at Gladstones, and I walk by a guy that is super cute. I turn around to check him out and realize it is Kurt Russell. At exactly the moment I turn around to look at him, he turns around to look at me, and our eyes meet. I imagine he is thinking, she looks just like Goldie. Goldie Hawn is another of my favorite stars from the eighties, and since junior high, people have been telling me that I look like her. Then I notice Goldie sitting across the table from him. I run back into the restaurant to the phone, and call my friend Smitty.

"Oh my gosh, you're not going to believe who is here. It's Goldie Hawn!"

"I'm coming down there. Don't let her leave," Smitty commands me.

Like I could stop her from leaving. What am I going to say? Excuse me, Goldie, but my friend Smitty is on her way, and I know you don't know her, but could you please stay for ten more minutes until she arrives so she can gawk at you and embarrass me completely?

Well my dear friend Smitty, crazy girl that she is, actually drives down to Gladstones. The truth is, she only lives about five minutes away, but still. She grabs me by the hand and walks straight up to Goldie.

"Everybody tells my friend that she looks just like you. I think she should be in a movie with you."

Goldie looks at me and says, "You *do* look like me."

She chats with us for a little bit and seems friendly and down to earth just like you'd expect her to be. It's so nice, and unusual, when you meet a celebrity and they are actually the same person they've portrayed themselves to be in the media. It is a memorable moment and means so much to me.

Some of the other celebrities I serve at Gladstones include: Magic Johnson, Stevie Wonder, Heather Locklear, Gene Simmons, Cindy Crawford, the cast from "Full House", Peter Reckle (Bo Brady on *Days of Our Lives*), Mark Harmon, and Dean Cain (oh my goodness, he is so cute).

At the end of my shift one day, I am looking down, focusing intently as I fill salt and pepper shakers, when a male hand slides a hundred dollar bill in front of me, and a familiar voice says, "Do you have change for this?"

I look up, into the brown eyes and smiling face of Erik Estrada. I feel faint.

"Of course I do! Anything for you, Erik," I say coyly, which brings a big smile to his face and use my tip money to give him change.

A hundred dollars is a lot of money, but I tuck the bill away in a zippered pocket in my wallet, promising to save it forever, because it was touched by Erik Estrada.

CHAPTER ELEVEN
Meeting the Kardashian Krew

The time I spend with Linda and the boys is a fraction of what it used to be. I am so busy during the week with school and my job at Gladstones that I hardly see them. I cherish my time with them on the weekends. Although it's difficult not having any time off, I miss them and enjoy their company.

In the summer of 1990, Sara marries her longtime boyfriend. I am the maid of honor in her wedding, held in Pasadena. We don't see each other much these days, as my schedule is so crazy, and she's busy with her new life. Her wedding day is a moment of reflection for me. Our lives have moved in different directions. I'm so busy that I don't have time for dating. I do want marriage and children some day. I know the day will come (probably sooner than I can imagine) when I begin to feel a strong pull to settle down. But for now, I don't even have time to think about it much. My life is full with school, work, and caring for Brandon and Brody.

I don't see Bruce much either. He's around occasionally on the weekends that I am working, and we still have our outings with the boys now and then, but not as often as we used to because I'm not the full-time nanny anymore. Part of me really misses that quality time the four of us used to have together and the constant of his friendship in my life. But, on the other hand, I'm thankful to be back in school, working, developing my own friendships with kids my age and enjoying a life outside of the Jenner family.

Not long before Christmas in 1990, I am studying in the guesthouse one evening, and Bruce pops his head in the door.

"Hey, Pam!"

I jump up from my books and give him a big hug. "Hey Bruce, how are you?" I ask.

"I'm really good. I went on a great date last night," he responds, with a glimmer in his eye that I have not seen before.

"Really? Do tell," I encourage him, a bit surprised by the excitement I see on his face.

"Her name is Kris. My buddy Steve set me up with her," Bruce shares with a big smile. I know he means Steve Garvey, a baseball player with the L.A. Dodgers, who is a friend. "We went on a blind date last night — out to eat — and I had a great time," he continues.

I am taken aback. I am surprised by the eagerness I see on his face, the excitement is his eyes, and the glow of his face. Bruce has dated here and there, and had a couple girlfriends since I started working for Linda, but nothing serious. I've certainly never seen him acting like this before. I want to know more.

"Well, tell me about her. What is she like?" I inquire.

"She is beautiful, smart, and funny. She has four kids — three girls and a boy. I think we really hit it off," he concludes with a grin.

I have a sinking feeling in my stomach that I will not be spending much more time with Bruce and the boys. I guess I'm a little jealous, but not because I want to be dating him. I just don't want our fun times together to end.

A few days after they meet, Bruce is at Linda's house again, talking about Kris. Disappointment or confusion obviously registers on my face. I feel like I am losing my best friend, and my feelings are impossible to hide. Bruce leans over and puts his arm around me, assuring, "Don't worry, Pam. If we get married, you are coming with us. I promise."

The comment is intended to make me feel better, but clarifies how serious he is about her, given that he is *already* thinking about marriage.

The next week, Bruce takes the boys and me by Kris's house in Beverly Hills, and I get the chance to meet her. She is not at all what I expect — the complete opposite of Linda. Kris's jet black hair is cut short in a very chic and sleek style. She is dressed in black from head to toe — black top, flowing black and blue skirt, and black leather cowboy boots with steel tips. She is beautiful, elegant, and sophisticated.

I also meet Kris's children for the first time, as I've mainly been brought along to keep an eye on all of the kids. They are gorgeous children — all have dark hair and dark eyes like their mom. Kourtney, the oldest, is eleven, and Kim just turned ten. They say hi and then run off to their rooms. The two little ones, Khloe, who is six, and Robert, who is almost four, are full of energy. The kids are a bit shy at first, but before long, Brandon, Brody, Khloe, and Robert are all playing well together.

On the drive home, Bruce asks me, "So what did you think of Kris?"

"I really like her. She seems great," I respond. "You seem very happy, and that's what is most important."

"Thanks, Pam. I am," Bruce says through a Cheshire Cat grin.

My gut feeling was right. Bruce starts seeing Kris regularly and spends most of his free time with her. Within a couple months, Bruce and Kris are engaged and planning a wedding. I learn from Bruce that Kris is soon to be divorced from Robert Kardashian, the father of the four kids, who is a prominent attorney and businessman.

Bruce tells me again that he wants me to be the nanny for Kris's kids and promises he will talk to her about it. Two and a half years have passed since I started working for Linda. I am only helping her two days per week and getting no pay for that. It is nice to have a place to live for free, but I really need more money to help pay my expensive tuition at Pepperdine.

Quitting my job with Linda is a tough decision, because I love her, Brandon, and Brody so much. They have become my family. I especially struggle with leaving the boys, but I rationalize that I will continue to see them regularly when they visit their dad.

Bruce comes by to tell me that Kris has agreed to hire me. She and I talk on the phone several times to make plans for my new schedule. I wonder how I will juggle school, my job at Gladstones, and time with the kids. My first impression of Kris over the phone is that she is sweet and friendly, but definitely has clear expectations, and no reservations about stating them.

Talking to Linda is difficult, but she understands how the new arrangement fits my needs better. Anne is happy to pick up some extra hours on the weekends once I am gone. So my absence will not cause a big disruption in the household.

I am emotional as I say goodbye to Linda and the boys. It is hard to leave the house, which has been my home for over two years. I expect to see Brandon and Brody often and promise Linda that I will come by and visit her soon.

CHAPTER TWELVE
Moving On Up to the Big Time

My first official day of work as nanny to the Kardashian kids is April 21, 1991 — the wedding day of Bruce and Kris. The outdoor wedding is held at a beautiful mansion in Bel Air (a very wealthy area of Los Angeles, even more exclusive than neighboring Beverly Hills). I am mesmerized by the beautiful people and extravagance. For a small town girl from Minnesota, the event and setting seem like a royal wedding. Every detail — from the flowers to the dresses to the table settings — is picture perfect.

The ceremony and reception are held outside in the expansive backyard that is meticulously landscaped. White and pink flowers are everywhere, and the fragrance in the air is heavenly. White chairs line the lawn in perfect rows on one side for the ceremony, while the other half of the yard holds tables that seem too beautiful to touch. They are works of art with crisp white linens, white china, exquisite crystal, and lovely centerpieces with aromatic white and pink blooms.

The event is quite a contrast to the weddings I've attended back in the Midwest. Most wedding receptions were held in the basement of a church or at the local American Legion (every town has one), with sandwiches, a few salads, and wedding cake served buffet style. Occasionally, someone would really go all out and hold the reception at a hotel in a neighboring town with a formal sit-down dinner. But that was a rarity. I had never been to a wedding like this before.

It is my responsibility to watch the kids before the ceremony and during the reception. Kourtney, Kim, and Khloe are wearing matching white dresses, with puffy sleeves, and a full, mid-calf length skirt. The beautiful garments are romantic and princess-like, and remind me of the dresses worn by the flower girls in Princess Diana's wedding a decade ago. Each girl wears a circular headpiece of white and pink flowers. Little Robert sports a mini black tuxedo and perfectly shined black shoes.

As I observe them and interact with them, I realize they each have unique and distinct personalities.

Kourtney, who just celebrated her twelfth birthday, is a serious child, and always speaks her mind. She is definitely the leader. She seems unhappy and acts distant towards me all day. I wonder what is going on with her.

Kim looks gorgeous. Even as a ten-year old child, she is stunning. She seems a bit on the quiet side but is sweet and friendly towards me.

Khloe is a pistol. Full of energy, with a long, thick mane of curly hair, she and Robert run all over the grounds of the mansion. Here it is my first day, and I envision having to explain to my new boss, Kris, why her daughter has a ripped dress with grass stains before the ceremony and pictures.

Little Robert is mostly sweet and precious, but he *is* a four year-old boy and has moments of mischievousness. He reminds me so much of "Charlie" from the movie *The Santa Claus* with Tim Allen. He has the same round "bowl" haircut, big brown eyes, and a sweet smile.

As the kids take their place (dresses and tuxedo intact and clean), and the ceremony begins, I sit in a back row, as questions and thoughts swirl through my mind. Will the kids like me? Can I handle four? Will Kris be a good boss? Can I manage being a nanny, attending school full-time, and working at Gladstones? I hope I am up to the task. I hope I've made the right decision.

As the reception winds down, I drive my four new charges home. What a huge and significant event for my initial day of work with my new family. I think to myself that it is appropriate that I get to share their "new beginning" with them. However, it is a lot of adjusting for everyone. New marriage, new step kids, the blending of three different sets of kids, *and* a new nanny. It is a lot for everyone to acclimate to and process.

I feel somewhat lost. After several years, I had a well-established routine with Brandon and Brody. They knew my boundaries and rules, and what was negotiable and what wasn't. Now, I am starting all over with *four* kids. It is not just double the work — it is more like quadruple the work.

I'm also dealing with the transition from boys who don't care what they have on, what they look like, or if they get dirty, to three girls who are

concerned with clothes, hair, and girly things. My tomboy background suited me well with Brandon and Brody. I was used to fishing, soccer, baseball, rough housing, and running around. It was more physical exertion. Now, I must put a lot more effort into emotional connections. Thank goodness I have little Robert who keeps me grounded.

I feel overwhelmed for the first few days. I am still acclimating to a new house, a new room, and a new bed, not to mention five new personalities. I'm thankful for Bruce's presence. For a while, though, I feel like a visitor.

Bruce and Kris recently purchased the Malibu home we all now share. There is a long sidewalk leading up to the front door, which opens into a spacious, bright, open foyer. The living room is straight ahead with floor to ceiling glass, offering a brilliant view of the ocean. The back yard, which is beautifully manicured, has a huge pool, a jacuzzi, and patio furniture that I'd love to sink into for a catnap in the sun (if I ever had the time). The marble floor in the foyer leads to a huge kitchen opening to a spacious family room. The home is warm, comfortable, tastefully decorated in a casual way. Not too pretentious or ostentatious.

I am thrilled to find out that Sean Penn used to own the house, during the time when he was dating Madonna. As I walk through the house, I feel reverent. I tread upon the same floors that were likely once graced by a music icon. When I'm home alone, I sing "Like a Prayer" and dance through the halls, wondering to myself if Madonna sang the same words to Sean right here in this house.

Bruce and Kris delay their honeymoon, but as a newlywed, Kris has many other things on her mind besides training me, which I completely understand. I am on my own for the first few days, so I wing it as best I can. Thankfully, a few days later, Kris makes time to go over my role, responsibilities, rules, and expectations. I make it clear to Kris that the most important priority in my life is school. We agree on a schedule that will work around my school commitments.

"Oh and I'll need you to cook dinner for us most nights. When Bruce and I are around, plan for ten," Kris adds, which sends shivers done my spine.

The only "cooking" I've done up until now was mainly for the boys. Simple kid food like Hamburger Helper, mac and cheese, hot dogs, and heating up food in the microwave.

Back in junior high school, I took a class called Home Economics, where Mrs. Oachs taught us how to be excellent housewives, but I never seemed able to get the hang of it. I burned the butterscotch pudding, made a cake that was flat as a pancake, and squeaked out a decent grade only because the cute yellow and white striped sundress I sewed was actually wearable, even though it had some crooked seams. That early experience haunts me. I guess I actually have a fear of failure when it comes to cooking.

"Kris, I hate to tell you this, but I don't really know how to cook," I say quietly, not sure how she will respond.

"What do you mean, you don't know how?" she asks, looking at me incredulously.

"Well, I can make mac and cheese, hamburger helper, hot dogs, fix lunches, heat up microwave meals, but I'm not like a chef or anything. I don't really know how to prepare gourmet meals." I'm talking quickly, nervous that she will be upset.

"Oh that's no problem," she says with a wave of her hand. "It doesn't have to be gourmet. I'll teach you some easy dishes."

And she does. We start with her favorite recipe, Pasta Primavera. She works with me in the kitchen, explaining each step. A few nights later, she shows me how to make barbeque chicken, baked potatoes, garlic cheese bread, and a mixed green salad with veggies. Before long, I have a whole repertoire of dishes: pasta with fresh tomato sauce and basil, noodles with broccoli and olive oil, homemade tacos, roasted chicken with vegetables, and spaghetti with meatballs.

Over the course of the next couple weeks, I develop a routine. My alarm goes off about five o' clock each morning. Crawling out of bed still half asleep, I shuffle into the kitchen in my pajamas and get the Starbucks Breakfast Blend brewing in the coffee maker. Kris asked me on my first day to prepare a tray with cups, cream and sugar, and a steaming carafe of coffee to leave outside their bedroom door each morning. I consider buying a hotel maid's outfit and getting one of those little signs you hang on the doorknob, so they can notify me when they need assistance or don't want to be disturbed. I think it would be funny, but they might not find it too amusing, so I drop the idea.

My "breakfast" is usually a cup of the Starbucks coffee and three or four vanilla sandwich cookies (one of the kids' favorites). I'm always running late and trying to get ten things done at once, so I don't have time to sit down and eat. We often keep fresh baked muffins in the kitchen, and occasionally I quickly grab the muffin top off to eat for my breakfast. This aggravates Bruce tremendously.

"Who took the muffin top?" I hear him yell from the kitchen. "Pam!"

Once I awaken all four kids, I then make sure the younger two are dressed. Kourtney and Kim wear uniforms (thank goodness or I can imagine we'd have a lot more drama in the mornings) and are independent enough to get themselves dressed, so I don't have to worry about that. I just need to make sure they are awake.

I help Khloe and Robert get something for breakfast, usually dry cereal, a muffin and fruit, or a bagel and cream cheese. While they eat breakfast, I pack their lunches. No two lunches are the same, as they each have "favorites" and certain things they dislike. I usually pack a sandwich, a piece of fruit, a bag

of chips, a juice box, and cookies. Khloe and Robert love Oreos, and Kourtney and Kim prefer the vanilla sandwich cookies. Next, I spend a few minutes going over the "to do" list for the day with Kris, who awakens early but spends the morning getting herself ready.

Kourtney and Kim spend all their time in the morning getting ready and usually grab something quick for breakfast on the way out the door, a muffin or a breakfast bar. Sometimes, they grab a bag of dry cereal and eat it in the car on the way to school. All five of us pile into the car, and we're on our way.

The three different schools they attend are *not* close in proximity. Although we live in Malibu, Kourtney and Kim attend a private school in Beverly Hills. After chauffeuring the older girls, I head back to Malibu to take Khloe to Kindergarten and Robert to preschool. Taking the four kids to their three different schools takes about an hour. Racing back to the house to drop off the car, I sprint up seven or eight flights of stairs at the University to try and make it to class on time. More often than not, I am late.

At noon every day, I leave Pepperdine, pick up the car, drive to the preschool and pick up Robert, drop him at home with the maid, and head back to class for the afternoon. When I finish my classes for the day, I get Robert and the car from the house, drive to Khloe's elementary school and scoop her up, and then drive back to Beverly Hills to pick up Kourtney and Kim at private school. Usually, Kris has given me a few errands to take care of before finally heading home.

My nanny job ends when the kids go to bed, which is about nine o'clock for Khloe and Robert, and around ten o'clock for Kourtney and Kim. But my day is not yet over. Exhausted as I may be since starting the day at five a.m., it is time to study. More often than not, I fall asleep with my head buried in a book. I'm surprised I get decent grades at Pepperdine, as little as I study.

My room at the Kardashian home used to be a storage room and pantry. It is about eight feet wide and ten feet long. The full sized bed fills most of the room with only about two feet on the edge of the bed. The room doesn't have a closet (it *is* a closet) or a desk, just a tiny little nightstand. It doesn't bother me though. I am rarely in my room, except for late at night. It is a place to study and sleep. Mostly sleep.

My list of duties also includes personal shopper. Once a week, usually on the weekend, I make a trip to the grocery store, and fill up two shopping carts full of food. Kris has a list of regular items that I am to purchase each week. In addition, I usually make one or two additional runs to the store during the week for special items or to stock up if we run out of a staple item.

After a disagreement one day over a missing item from the grocery list — broccoli — the tension in the room is so thick you can almost see it. I think to myself, Oh my gosh, what have I done? Why am I here? This lady really doesn't like me. During my conservative Midwest upbringing with a prim and proper mother, I'd *never* heard a lady talk to me the way she just did. I am quite certain I've made a huge mistake in coming to work for Kris and mentally start packing my bags. However, I have four kids who are depending on me, and it is important for me to be a stable force in their lives. I resolve not to let Kris get to me. But given the way Kris has just reacted about something as seemingly non-important as broccoli, I decide that isn't realistic, so for the time being I settle on not quitting...yet.

The next day, Kris apologizes, I think. If you can call it an apology.

"Are you mad at me, Pam? Wouldn't you rather I speak my mind and be done with it? Or would you rather have me act like nothing is wrong, when there *is* something wrong?"

I don't know how to respond. In her mind, her actions are completely rational. To me, her response to the "missing broccoli" is utterly irrational.

I am beginning to realize that Kris says what is on her mind in the moment that it happens. Whatever she is feeling, she communicates it — good, bad, or ugly. She is a perfectionist, very detail oriented, and has high expectations. She doesn't hold back.

I must admit, though, it is probably better for her to vent rather than feel the retribution of resentment later. Nevertheless, these moments when she "speaks her mind" can be tough to take. I am an emotional person, and I'm still just a kid.

I feel like I am trying so hard all of the time, and she doesn't recognize my effort. She points out the failures but doesn't compliment the good things I am doing.

Along with my nanny duties, I am also Kris's "personal assistant," which means taking care of all the errands and tasks it takes to run a household so she can focus on business projects for Bruce and herself.

I never know each day what I will be doing or where I will be going, only that I have to get everything on my "to do" list done. Which amounts to a great deal of pressure, considering I also have four kids to take care of, a full schedule of college courses, and a second job. Thank goodness I am young and have a lot of energy. Even so, I'm sure I am single-handedly increasing the stock price of Starbucks with all the coffee I drink.

Despite how challenging it is at times to be working for Kris, there are many things I admire about her. I have never before been around such a driven and savvy businesswoman. I look up to her and learn a lot from her. Growing up in a small town in a rural area, I had not been exposed to any strong businesswomen as role models, so it is quite amazing to watch Kris in action. When she puts her mind to something, she does not stop until she has accomplished what she set out to do. She is tenacious and does not take "no" for an answer. I'm not used to working for someone who sets the bar so high — for herself and for me. There are occasions I end up in tears.

Maybe she thinks I don't take her list seriously, which is not the case. I feel anxiety during the day as unforeseen obstacles like traffic interfere. I'm a people pleaser, and when I fail, it really bothers me.

It is becoming clear to me that life in this home is going to be busy, fun, and exciting, with never a dull moment, but also *extremely* challenging at times.

Because Bruce and Kris travel so much, they need someone at home to watch the kids and manage the household. I realize, as their nanny, I am not just a caretaker, but I am also a surrogate mom in a way. I fell in love with these kids very quickly, and I now love them as if they are my own. I assume, and hope, that's what Kris wants.

I allow myself to feel like a member of the family, because for the most part, Bruce and Kris treat me as such. There are times, however, when I have to remind myself that I am *not* a family member. I am paid (and paid well) to do this job. It is a strange dichotomy, this nanny thing. Live with the family full time, love the kids, pour yourself into them, spend every spare moment of your life taking care of them and their needs, but don't forget, when it comes down to it, you're just the nanny. Allowing my emotions to become too invested or expecting to be treated as an equal member of the family would most assuredly end in hurt feelings, so I attempt to keep my status and position in the forefront of my mind.

I reflect on the list of rules I wrote on the bus a couple of years ago, as I was about to meet Linda Jenner. I assumed that if I stuck to this list, I would be successful, my employers would be happy with me, and the kids would be content and well behaved.

After my first few months at the Kardashian home, I have one more rule to add to the top of that list.

1. Do not EVER forget the broccoli.

CHAPTER THIRTEEN
Elephants on Desks and Guns in the Trunk

It takes some getting used to the craziness of the Kardashian household. With four active and energetic kids, Bruce and Kris, myself, the maid, and usually a couple of friends running around, the house always seems full. The kids are still adjusting to the divorce of their mom and dad, while accepting a new stepfather *and* a new nanny.

Kourtney seems to be having the most difficult time with the changes. She is very straightforward and has a strong personality, just like her mom. I think because she is the oldest, she is the most responsible. She is wise beyond her years, with good common sense and a mature knowledge of right and wrong.

She seems standoffish towards Bruce. I realize she is disappointed about the divorce and not at all happy about this new marriage, which dashes her hopes that her mom and dad will get back together. Kris and Bruce met only five months before the wedding, and Kris's divorce from Robert was finalized the month before they married. Kourtney hasn't had a lot of time to grieve, process, and adjust to all of the changes happening in her life.

Bruce regularly tries to engage with Kourtney and to parent her as a good stepfather would. Kourtney wants nothing to do with it. One day, as Bruce tries to talk to Kourtney, she yells at him, "You're not my dad. Don't even talk to me!"

I feel bad for both of them. I wish I knew what to say to make her feel better, but this is all new for me too. I don't have any words of wisdom that will make it better. It must be heart-breaking to go through a divorce. Kourtney adores her father, and she is having a really difficult time being away from him so much. I can only hope and pray that time will heal the wounds and knit this family together.

Kim, sleeping beauty that she is, sometimes talks in her sleep. I find this quite amusing, and because I am a practical joker, I take the opportunity to have some fun with her. Sometimes, as I am checking to make sure she is asleep, I hear her talking.

One night she says, "There's an elephant on my desk."

I reply, "Well, get it off."

Kim moans, "Help me. Help me. Get it off."

I stifle a laugh, and rush out the door, before doubling over with laughter in the hallway.

Another night, she mumbles, "The guns are in the trunk."

"What are they doing in the trunk?" I ask.

"Kourtney put them there. Tell Mom!" Kim exclaims, and then rolls over.

As far as I know, they don't own any guns, so I'm not sure what she is talking about. She must have been watching a movie or television show that triggered those thoughts.

I learn quickly that Kim hates all bugs but especially spiders. She is deathly afraid of them and screams whenever she sees one. One day, I hear her shrieking — her voice full of panic. I run to her room, afraid something horrible has happened. She is standing on her bed, screaming and pointing at a huge spider on the floor. I kill it with my shoe and throw it in the toilet.

Kim enjoys making jewelry and has big cases full of beads of every size, shape, and color. She makes necklaces, bracelets, and earrings, spending countless hours in her room beading.

I love all four kids dearly, but I have developed a special bond with Khloe. She is at a very impressionable age, and I spend more time with her than any other adult. Khloe has lighter hair and complexion than her siblings and with our long curly hair, we look somewhat alike. I fix her hair just like mine. She has incredibly thick curly hair, and even if we use half a bottle of conditioner, it still takes forever to comb through her hair. She wants to be doing whatever I am doing. If I'm washing the dishes, she is right beside me helping me dry. If I am cleaning the table, she has a rag in her hand helping me. Khloe is my little sidekick, and I love it.

One day, Kris has some girlfriends over, and one of them who has been watching Khloe and me together, whispers, "Khloe could be yours." I smile, but don't say anything (I don't dare for fear of it being repeated to Kris), but it is a great compliment. I love that Khloe not only looks like me, but wants to copy my every move.

One of my biggest challenges from the very first week has been getting Khloe to school. She absolutely hates school. Every single morning, she has a new and different excuse for why she can't make it to class.

"Pam, I have a headache. I can't go to school," she tells me one morning.

"Okay, I'll get you some Tylenol and a glass of water," I say. "Please get dressed, Khloe, and come and eat breakfast."

The next day it is something different. "I have a horrible stomach ache," she moans, as if she is about to die. "I'm so sick, I can't make it to school."

"You are not going to die, Khloe. If you have a tummy ache, I'll get you some Pepto Bismol." I say firmly. "Please get ready. You are going to school."

It is more of the same the next day. "I didn't get my homework done. I better not go to school," she whines. "The teacher will be so mad at me."

"Khloe! You are going to school."

It is a struggle each and every day to get her up and ready and on her way to school. I always wake Khloe first and have to focus a great deal of my time on her, because it takes so much effort to get that kid out the door.

Khloe's favorite movie is *Grease* and often I catch her standing on the coffee table "stage" in the living room, dancing and singing the songs from the movie. She pleads with her mom that she wants to learn to ice skate, so I drive her to lessons several times each week.

I love country western music. I play it at the house whenever I am in control of the radio, and, when I tire of my Madonna, the Beach Boys, and Def Leppard cassettes in the car, I tune into a country radio station. Kris and the older girls can't stand country, and they always make me turn it off, but Khloe and Robert love it. One of our favorite country songs is "The Auctioneer Song." The chorus goes something like this, "Sold to the lady in the second row. She's an eight, she's a nine, she's a ten I know." Little Robert changes the words and sings, "Fart on the lady in the second row..." and the three of us roll on the floor with laughter.

Robert is a unique child, very self-motivated, and self-disciplined. He comes home from school and goes straight to his room to do his homework without being told. He then picks out his clothes for the next day. Once those tasks are complete, only then will he

allow himself to play. I've never known another four year-old child that is so responsible.

Despite his serious side, he is a typical little boy, teasing his big sisters and being a little goof ball. He has hamsters in his room, and they smell *so* bad. Of course, I get to clean their cage.

Robert has bunk beds in his room, and when it is bedtime, he begs me to lie in the bunk next to him. He bribes me by saying, "Pam, we can watch *I Love Lucy*."

He knows it is one of my favorite television shows and a sure way to get me to stay in his room longer.

Robert loves Kiki, his blanket that has been his constant companion for years. She is old, tattered, worn, dingy, and faded — but Robert loves her. One day, as I drop him off at preschool, the teacher introduces him to a new student.

"Hi Robert. This is your new classmate. Her name is Kiki."

Robert looks at me with a grimace on his face. He doesn't have to say a word. With a pleading expression in his eyes, he begs me not to say anything to the teacher or the girl. I smile back at him with a nod, promising silently to keep his secret.

CHAPTER FOURTEEN
A Hard Lesson

Near the end of my first summer with Bruce and Kris, I am finishing a shift at Gladstones. It has been a long day in the hot sun, and I am tired, my feet hurt, and I look forward to heading home to relax. But one of my co-workers is quitting, and there is a going away party at a nightclub in Santa Monica. He has been a good friend of mine at work, so I feel obligated to attend.

It is so rare that I have time to socialize with my friends outside of work and school, and even more rare that I am drinking when I do. Happy to be hanging out, I get caught up in the celebratory spirit of the evening, and when a friend orders me a second beer, I accept it and drink it.

Because I am truly exhausted and have to get up early the next morning (because I *never* sleep in), I excuse myself, and head to my car.

The thought crosses my mind, I wish I'd had only one beer. But now what do I do? I have several options. Wake up Bruce, wake up Smitty, or call a cab. All of these options involve 1) inconveniencing someone else, 2) leaving my car in Santa Monica, and 3) requiring the assistance of someone in the morning to retrieve it. I have to be at work early. It is so much easier to just drive home. I feel fine, I tell myself. I've only had two beers. I'm not drunk.

And I make the fateful decision to drink and drive.

The Pacific Coast Highway follows the coastline through Malibu and has one windy curve after another, for miles on end. It is late, and there is not a car on the road. I am so tired and not very careful as I take the curves to ensure that I stay in my lane. Dumb. Of course, I am pulled over by the highway patrol that wisely waits for inebriated souls driving home late at night that can't stay in their own lane.

As the flashing lights pull up behind me, and the siren wails, I chastise myself for driving so erratically when I have been drinking. Despite this, I am not too concerned, knowing that I've only had two beers. I doubt that I will be at the legal limit of .08 Blood Alcohol Content.

The cop's breathalyzer doesn't work. So I have the privilege of trying to perform the "drunk test" that no sane and sober person could ever pass. He doesn't tell me whether I pass or fail, but I must have gotten an "F," because he put me in his cop car and took me to the Malibu police station. They perform a breath analysis on me, and I blow .08 on the first test, and .07 on the second. They stick me in their cold, uncomfortable jail cell (even in exclusive Malibu the jail cells are cold and uncomfortable) for a few hours to sober up, and then book me for a violation of California Vehicle Code 23152 — aka, a DUI.

The arresting officer informs me, "Technically, Ms. Behan, we are supposed to take you to East L.A., and they should book you into jail there, because we don't have a female deputy on duty here."

For just a second, I get scared. East L.A. I've heard about East L.A. That's where the gang bangers live. Not a pretty place. Not a safe place.

But before I can protest, the officer continues, "Frankly, I would be scared about your safety there. As you may know, East L.A. is not like Malibu."

I look up at him, even more afraid, and not sure what he is planning.

"I'll bring you to the Jenner home." I had told him where I lived, and who I worked for. Whether it made a difference, I'm not sure. But I figured in the circumstances I was in, if name-dropping might help even the slightest bit, well I was certainly going to try.

"But, Ms. Behan," he says sternly. "I'd better not see your car moved from that spot tonight, or I will arrest you again tomorrow. "

The next morning, I have to put my tail between my legs, suck up my pride, and tell Bruce that not only did I get a DUI, but I also need a ride back to my car. With a shocked expression on his face, he says simply, "What?!"

He is obviously very surprised, because he's known me for three years, and I've never gotten into trouble before. He doesn't seem angry but rather just shocked.

I apologize profusely to Bruce. I don't want him or Kris to think I am irresponsible or to have any concerns about my ability to care for their children. I am angry at myself for my lapse in judgment. I ask him to trust that I have learned my lesson, and I will never take that risk again. I feel shameful about my lack of maturity.

A few days later, I go to court and fight the DUI on the basis that one of my breathalyzer tests was below .08%, and I wasn't given a breathalyzer in the field. Fortunately, I am able to have the charge removed from my record.

I learn a valuable lesson that night. It only takes two beers to reach the level of being "legally impaired," and although I may feel like I'm capable of driving, it is *never* worth the risk to myself, the lives of others, or my future.

I promise myself, no more mess-ups.

CHAPTER FIFTEEN
Miss Minnesota and Dr. Sex

After enjoying a break from the crazy morning routine during summer vacation, school starts again in September. I hate being late to my college classes, but I can't help it, and it has become a daily occurrence. Whether it's the dog needing to be let out and fed, Robert spilling breakfast on his shirt and having to change, the older girls having a fight, someone forgetting their homework, or bad traffic on the freeways — there is always something that seems to happen to get me off schedule.

I am particularly upset that I am always late to my first class, because I have a crush on my professor, Dr. Sexton (his actual name, for which I am sure he was mercilessly teased as a child). Incidentally, I realize that my "love life" seems to consist of one crush after another. Rarely does it move beyond a crush. I chalk that up to the reality that I have no time for dating. At least, I hope that's the issue, and not a statement about my potential as a dating partner, nor a comment about my looks or personality.

Anyway, after numerous days of being late, my latest crush decides that he has had enough. As I walk in (late again) one morning, Dr. Sexton asks, in front of an auditorium filled with students, "Where are you from?"

"Minnesota," I reply, completely embarrassed.

"Miss Minnesota, why are you always late for class?" he asks.

"I'm sorry, but I'm a nanny and I have to take four kids to school every morning, and two of them go to school in Beverly Hills." I explain sheepishly, hoping that he will be understanding and go easy on me.

"Okay then," is all he says.

Every day after that, as I stride in, late as usual, he welcomes me to class by saying, "Hello, Miss Minnesota" or "Welcome, Miss Minnesota" or "Thanks for joining us, Miss Minnesota."

I love it, because he is gorgeous, and I love the attention.

A few days later, I am in the school cafeteria, on a break between classes, looking for a place to sit. In one hand, I hold a drink I have just purchased, in the other, a stack of books. As I lift the cup to my mouth to take a drink, the straw goes up my nose. When I pull the cup away, the straw stays in my nose, and of course, at that very moment Dr. Sexton walks in the door. He looks at me with a puzzled expression and inquires, "What are you doing now, Miss Minnesota?"

I want to disappear.

CHAPTER SIXTEEN
Kris-mas

With the holidays right around the corner, I learn that Christmas is a festive, all out production at the Kardashian/Jenner home.

Right after Thanksgiving, Kris hires someone to put up a large Christmas tree in the living room and decorate it perfectly. Decorations throughout the entire house match the theme of the tree. White lights twinkle everywhere in the front yard. It is a "Kris-mas" Wonderland.

Kris started a tradition back when the kids were really small to take a formal photo for their Christmas cards each year. She chooses a theme, and everyone in the family dresses up accordingly. The theme for this year is black and white, with Teenage Mutant Ninja Turtles. I set aside an entire day and run all over town finding the "perfect" outfits for all four kids, plus Brandon, Brody, Burt, and Casey, who will also be in the picture. Kris gives me a list of the styles and sizes she wants, and I spend a day shopping to track everything down.

It seems like shopping is my full-time job the few weeks before I head home for Christmas. It is actually rather fun playing Santa's little helper. The sauna tub in Bruce and Kris's master bath is heaped full of toys for the kids by the time I am finished, and the master bedroom suite is strictly off limits for them.

It takes me a day and a half to perfectly (and I mean perfectly) and festively wrap each and every one of the presents. Kris has purchased wrapping paper that matches the theme of the tree and several rolls of inch wide silk ribbon — the kind with wire in the edges, so I can make perfect bows. I really enjoy the gift wrapping, as it's a nice break from the normal routine. I crank up the Christmas music, grab a Snapple and some snacks, and lock myself in the master bedroom.

Every now and then I hear a knock.

"Pam?" a small voice pipes up from behind the door.

"Yes, Khloe, what is it?"

"I really need something from mom's bathroom. Can I come in?"

"No Khloe. You are not allowed in here. What do you need? I'll get it for you," I reply.

It becomes a game among the kids to see who can get into the bedroom to spy on the presents.

A few weeks before Christmas, Bruce and Kris throw a holiday party for a small group of close friends. They ask me to provide entertainment for the gathering, and so I play about thirty minutes of Christmas songs. One of my favorites is "Night of Silence," a rendition of the traditional Christmas song, "Silent Night." The party is festive and fun, and really gets me in the holiday spirit. I feel sentimental and I'm missing my Mom and Dad.

I spend a week back in Norcross with my family for the holidays. I am so exhausted from my crazy schedule, I spend a lot of time sleeping. It is so nice to have my mom doting on me, making home cooked meals, and connecting with my family and dear friends. Sara is home for Christmas too with her husband. We spend a day together and comment how sad it is that we don't get together more often. With my crazy schedule and her new marriage, we rarely see each other.

When I return from my much needed break, Khloe and Robert are excited to show me their favorite Christmas present — a black lab puppy named Harley. I am thrilled to meet Harley too because of my love for labs. Unfortunately, though, it does mean even more work for me. Add these to my list of "personal assistant" duties: dog watcher, dog walker, dog poop cleaner-upper.

A few weeks later, I tell my friend Chad (my other close friend from Pepperdine, whom I met at Orientation) that the Kardashians got a black lab puppy for Christmas. He loves dogs and comes by the house a few days later to meet him. He gets so attached to Harley that he begs me to let him take the puppy back to his dorm room for the night. I caution him that it's not a good idea, because Harley still whines a lot at night. But he insists.

At five a.m. the next morning, the phone rings at the Jenner home just as I am putting on the pot of coffee.

"Pam?" whispers a strained voice. "It's Chad. You have to come and get Harley right now. He cried and whined the entire night. I haven't slept at all."

"I told you so," I remind him, and drive over to get the pup, who's happy to come back to his home and new family.

As I'm watching Khloe play with Harley a few days later, I realize I shouldn't have allowed Chad to talk me into taking the pup. It was somewhat irresponsible of me. What if something had happened to Harley? Khloe would have been devastated.

One day, when I pick Khloe up from school, she excitedly tells me she has a surprise for me. She pulls something out of her school bag and places it in my hands. It is a ceramic cocker spaniel figurine that she has obviously painted herself.

"We did this in class. We got to pick what kind of animal we wanted, so I picked a dog. And I want you to have it because I know you like dogs too. I made it for you," she explains with a big smile on her face.

"Thank you so much, Khloe," I respond, tearing up. "I love it."

And I really do. She seems pleased that I've gotten emotional about it. It touches me that she thought of me. I place it next to my bed when I get home. I will save this forever, I think. It will always remind me of my special bond with Khloe.

I drive a lovely, old paneled station wagon *exactly* like the one I had at Linda's. What is it with nannies and old station wagons? I feel like such a dork driving that car around, but we sure do have fun.

When I pick Khloe up from school, she often has a frown on her face, because she doesn't like school. She always wants to sit next to me in the front passenger seat. I rub her arm and wrist as we drive to pick up the older girls. When I stop, she says, "Keep doing that." She almost falls asleep. I love this little girl so much.

The station wagon has a cassette tape player, and I play my three tapes for the kids. When the kids get really tired of those songs, I turn on the radio. I love Gloria Estefan's song called "I Live for Loving You." Whenever it comes on, I turn it up real loud and sing along. Kim and Kourtney hate it.

"Pam, you are such a nerd," Kourtney always says.

I respond, "Someday when I'm gone, you'll hear this song, and you'll think of your old Nanny Pam."

We spend a tremendous amount of time in the car together. We usually listen to music, but also play games or just talk about life. It is a great bonding time with all four kids.

On Fridays, I bring the kids to Baskin Robbins for ice cream cones. Kourtney and Kim always get frozen yogurt. Khloe likes bubble gum or cotton candy, and Robert asks for plain old vanilla. I wonder what their ice cream choices say about their personalities and who they will be some day?

We make many great memories in the clunker station wagon, but I always grimace a bit when I drive through the Malibu streets, seeing luxury cars left and right, and as I park next to Bruce's BMW. There is another older car parked at their Malibu house that doesn't quite fit into the neighborhood either. Bruce has a junky old van that he used to haul around the go-karts that he often rode with Brandon and Brody. It becomes a bit of a joke between

Kris and me, as we both think the van is so awful. She plots with me how to get rid of it.

She says, "Pam, put the pedal to the medal and run that thing right off the cliff into the ocean. Just jump out quick!"

And we laugh hysterically. I also hear her scheming with friends, asking them to steal it and never bring it back. Needless to say, the van doesn't stay around for long, and the go-kart racing seems to stop too.

I continue to try to figure Kris out. She seems to so easily juggle motherhood, marriage, and business, and has extremely high expectations for me. She is an intense person, and as the matriarch, she sets the tone of the household. Everyone speaks exactly what is on his or her mind, and the home seems chaotic to me at times, which is not how I was raised. My house was fairly quiet and civilized, not much yelling or craziness. Especially when I return from a visit back home, the differences stand out. I realize, however, that this is my new normal and learn to adapt to the chaos and not let it bother me.

Kris expects me to run a tight ship. It is *not* okay to run out of something, like broccoli for example, with no back up. Sometimes I have no control over the situation, because one of the kids uses the last of something and doesn't tell me. But Kris enforces a "no excuses" policy, even for situations like the cleaners being closed, not having a receipt for a return, or the notoriously horrible Los Angeles traffic that causes me to be late.

Kris wants what she wants when she wants it, which is usually "now." I try hard to please her. She likes to make lists, and I like to check things off my list. The perfectionist in me wants to make sure I get every last thing done, even if it kills me.

There are days, however, that no matter how hard I try, I can't give her what she wants. One morning, I accidentally break the glass carafe of the coffee maker. I spend an entire afternoon running all over Los Angeles trying in vain to find a replacement carafe, because she doesn't want to buy a new coffee maker. I never do find one.

I wonder to myself if her lack of praise is a choice. Maybe it's her management style. I never hear words of appreciation. A top-notch effort is expected, bottom line. Maybe she feels that if she tells me I'm doing a good job, I might not work as hard.

In spite of my frustration at times, I do love Kris, and I enjoy working for her. I also love a challenge, and every single day I face a new and exciting challenge. Maybe love isn't the right word here. Accept might fit a bit better. I accept the new challenge.

Bruce is very laid back, and brings a sense of calm and normalcy to the house. Bruce always works hard and is on the road constantly making motivational speeches. He has become quite involved in the lives of the four Kardashian kids, wanting to know what they are doing, and chatting with them often about their lives and what is going on with them. He is a good stepfather and a stable force in their lives.

Although Kourtney had a difficult time accepting Bruce as her stepfather initially, she eventually starts to see that Bruce is a really nice guy and truly cares about her and her siblings. As Kourtney learns she can trust him, she starts to confide in him. Bruce is a good role model for the kids and is always positive and inspirational. He really understands people, how to motivate them, and how to communicate with them. The role Bruce seems to hold in the family is peacemaker.

Bruce and Kris are yin and yang, differing personalities that somehow make it work. I guess opposites do attract. Kris seems more driven and organized, while Bruce is so laid back. Maybe the draw between them was their family orientation — they each had four kids when they met. Bruce and Kris both have a "no excuses" attitude when it comes to setting and achieving goals. Maybe that's the big connection. It has made them good business partners. They understand each other on that level. Don't make excuses. Just do what you have to do to reach your goal.

Kris loves fashion and always looks very nice. Her overflowing closet and shopping habits seem pretty extravagant to a small town girl from the Midwest. Also, she spends what to me seems like an insane amount of money each week for fresh cut flowers for the house, whether company is expected or not. However, the house always looks beautiful. It is stylishly decorated, perfectly clean and orderly at all times, and the sweet smell of fresh flowers permeates throughout. I must admit it is a lovely environment in which to live and work.

I am about the same size as Kris, and I get a lot of hand me downs from her, which is incredibly generous, although not a very realistic wardrobe for a nanny who spends her time in the car pool lane, at the grocery store, and sitting in a classroom on a college campus. Where on earth am I going to wear a red leather dress? I have inherited two of those leather dresses — a black one as well.

Kris loves to shop and often goes out for lunch or shopping with her girlfriends. La Scala restaurant, in Beverly Hills, is one of Kris's favorite spots, and she goes to lunch there regularly. I've been there many times picking up her favorite takeout lunch — their chopped salad and fresh warm bread.

Bruce loves to golf, which he does whenever he has free time. He also likes to race remote control vehicles. There always seems to be an RC car or helicopter buzzing around the yard. Bruce also spends time with a pal named Dean, who is a helicopter pilot. They share a love of flying.

I find it surprising that an Olympic gold medal winner is not really into working out. He is active, but he doesn't do regular gym workouts. He prefers to golf, bike, hike, or walk. He says that when he won the Olympics he told himself that he would never work out another day in his life, because he was so sick of it.

Despite their individual interests, Bruce and Kris also make time for regular date nights. They often go out for dinner, dressed in evening attire.

Kris is more often than not wearing black and always looks perfectly put together — hair, nails, makeup, jewelry, and her latest high fashion find.

One night Bruce and Kris are heading out for a night on the town, and Kris is draped in a gorgeous mink fur coat. I have to turn away to hide my smile, because the thought occurs to me that one of the minks in her coat might have been trapped by my father. I imagine how horrified she might be if she could see me scraping the fat off of a mink skin with a big spoon. It is one of those moments when the chasm between Beverly Hills and rural Minnesota seems insurmountable.

Bruce and Kris also like to take rides on their Harley Davidson motorcycles. (Kris just got hers recently.) One afternoon, they take off for a ride together. Returning a few hours later, Kris is obviously unhappy. Bruce tells me how, while stopped at a major intersection in Beverly Hills, Kris dropped the bike (a biker term that means the bike fell over). She is incredibly embarrassed, and the motorcycle is relegated to a corner in the garage. Before long, the bike is sold.

Bruce and Kris travel quite often, as Bruce has speaking engagements all over the United States. Kris works hard at crafting Bruce's career, networking constantly to establish speaking engagements. Also, Bruce is spokesperson for a company that owns a number of fitness centers, Bruce Jenner's Westwood Centers, which Kris helps to promote. So they are often on the road. When she is home, Kris spends most of her day in the office, marketing Bruce and the fitness company, as well as planning all of her appointments. That woman has more appointments than anyone I've ever known. Business appointments, hair appointments, nail appointments, waxing appointments, massage appointments, lunch appointments, appointments with caterers (she *is* a great party planner and hostess), not to mention the play dates she plans for the kids.

Because Bruce and Kris travel so much, the kids and I are often alone in the evenings. From day one, I consider it my responsibility to teach the Kardashian kids the same values and work ethic that I learned in my childhood in Minnesota. My parents taught me how to work hard, be responsible, and contribute to the family. Whenever the opportunity presents itself, I give the four kids chores and duties, have them clean up after themselves, and try to teach them that the world doesn't revolve around them. I strive to create boundaries and rules.

One night, shortly after Bruce and Kris return home from a trip, Kris hands the kids candy right before dinner. Khloe says "We can't have that right now."

Kris looks at me and then at the kids and replies, "What do you mean you can't have that right now? Of course you can have that right now."

I feel undermined but try to see it through her eyes. I realize she has been gone, and she wants to bring her kids a treat. The mother/nanny relationship can be tenuous at times because we both love the kids, but sometimes we have different priorities. Because they are often gone, Kris sometimes doesn't know the nuances of my relationship with the kids or the rules and responsibilities I am trying to instill. Kris parents with a different set of rules than the ones I use to manage the kids when she is away. They are her kids, so of course I have no right to say anything to her (or even to be upset about it), but, I must admit, it does bother me at times. I feel like she is stepping on my toes when situations like that occur.

The kids go to the Beverly Hills home of their dad, Robert, every other weekend, so I have kept the job at Gladstones and wait tables on those weekends I have off. Occasionally, the schedule changes, and the kids are at the house on the weekend I am working. I made an agreement with Kris up front that I will *not* change my schedule last minute, because I will lose my job at Gladstones for cancelling without sufficient notice. As a result, these weekends "off" look a bit different than I would hope. When I get home, the kids are there, and without any formal discussion about it, they become my responsibility for the evening.

After a long, busy day on my feet, I just want to relax. I'm happy to see the kids, because I love them and I miss them when I am away, but it would be nice to have a breather. I never have much time to restore myself.

Despite the many distractions of my two jobs and my limited free time, college is serious business to me and is my priority. I struggle, however, to keep up with all of my coursework and studying. I squeeze it in whenever I can between my nanny job and working at Gladstones. Because I am a music major, I must practice and memorize pieces of music, in addition to my other coursework. I fit in practice time during the day at school as much as I can. Late evenings are reserved for reading and homework. Every moment of every day is accounted for. I do a fairly good job of finishing Kris's "to do" list every day, but my own list is long and often left undone.

March 1992
Dear Mom,

Happy Birthday! I wish I could be with you and spend the whole day together, maybe go shopping and out to eat. I would die to do that right now. I am so stressed out. I have my pre-recital in a week, in which all of the music staff listens to my memorized program and decides whether or not I'm able to do it. I'm almost ready, but I still have a little memorizing and perfecting to do. But Dolfie the maid is quitting today and I'll be on my own here for a week. What great timing, eh? On top of all that, the kids are having friends over night this weekend. My grades have been falling because of my lack of free time, and working every spare minute. Let's just say I'm very anxious for this week to be over. Well, I better go now but I sincerely hope you have a great birthday and remember that...

I love you!
Pam

One day I am driving the older girls somewhere in the old station wagon, and I allow them to pick the music. The only "music" they want to listen to these days is rap. I start rapping along with the lyrics for one of the tracks, "As I walk through the valley of the shadow of death."

"Pam, how do you know this song?" Kourtney asks, with an astonished look on her face.

"Because it's from the Bible. Psalm 23 is one of the most famous chapters in the Bible."

I am surprised they don't know that verse, since they attend a Catholic school. As I drive, I think about the valley I am going through. I haven't been to church in several years. I am drifting from God. Recently, during a phone conversation with my mom, she said, "Pam, you're changing."

After the phone call, her comment haunted me. I've thought about it many times. I don't read the Bible, I don't pray, and I'm not going to church. Maybe I've gotten caught up in the lifestyle around me. It seems that what I wear and what I drive is more important to me. I want to keep God number one in my life, but the reality is He has slipped to second or third. Maybe I should find another job or move back home. If the pull of this lifestyle is affecting me enough that my mom is noticing, maybe it's not the right thing for me.

CHAPTER SEVENTEEN
Vin Rouge

I am usually so busy I don't have much time to socialize with friends. Thankfully, I have some friends who drag me out every now and then. Smitty loves a good party but particularly Halloween. We went to a party together last year, and now she wants me to go with her this year as well. I protest, telling her I'm too exhausted. She keeps calling, begging me to join her. I think I've won my case, and I'm settling in for a nice quiet evening at home with a movie, since the kids are at their dad's house and Bruce and Kris are away.

I hear a knock on the door, and it's Smitty with a big grin on her face. I can't say no to someone who puts in that much effort. Smitty is dressed as a lobotomy patient, with a homemade tag that says, "Pepperdine Psych Ward." If I'm going out, I need a costume. We search through the house, poking through the kids' closets to find something we can make into a costume for me. I find a really long wig in Kourtney's closet. It will have to do. I plaster my hair back with bobby pins and hair gel, put on some garish makeup, a black dress and heels, and we are good to go.

A few hours later, we are reveling with the masses at a house party near UCLA. The house is so packed and hot Smitty and I escape to the upstairs balcony overlooking the living room to catch our breath and get some air. My throat is parched, and it is my turn to get us drinks, so I head back down stairs, grab two sodas, and then turn to make my way back across the jammed "dance floor" with a can in each hand. Unfortunately, my long wig, which hangs down past my butt, catches on something. I keep going, but my wig does not. There I stand with my hair a plastered mess of gel and bobby pins.

I am mortified and try in vain to grasp both sodas in one hand while picking up my wig. I spill Coke all over myself, but finally manage to grab the errant wig, which I plop back on my head, not caring that it is terribly askew. So much for any hopes of meeting a hot guy at *this* college party. As I stand up, I see Smitty up on the balcony, grabbing her stomach, doubled over in fits of laughter.

Bruce and Kris return from their trip, and since I recently celebrated a birthday, Kris presents me with a beautifully wrapped gift. Opening it, I gasp with surprise to find a soft, black leather Chanel backpack and organizer. I am floored by their generosity, which I interpret to mean that she is pleased with the job I am doing. I've noticed that Kris often shows her appreciation with money.

A couple months later, I am at work at Gladstones and park my car across the street, because employees are not allowed to park in the parking lot. After work, I walk back to my car. When I try to unlock it, I realize the door is already open. I can't remember if I locked it or not. I usually do. I notice the faint clicking of the motor — the same sound it makes after it has been turned off. I walk over and touch the hood. It is warm. I open the door and look inside. My Chanel bag, which I left in the car, is gone.

I am shaken. I had the keys with me. How could someone have started my car? They must have hot wired it. Where did they take it?

I drive home, and Kris is in the kitchen. She can tell I am upset and asks me what is wrong. I explain what happened and admit the Chanel backpack was in the car and has been stolen. She empathizes with me and helps me to calm down.

A few days later, Kris comes home one day, and presents me with a brand new Chanel backpack and organizer. I am shocked. It is a thoughtful and kind gesture.

At times like this, I see the soft side of Kris and her warm heart. She even confides in me occasionally, and there are fleeting moments when I feel like a close friend.

I notice that Kris is not as uptight when she's had a glass or two of wine. It seems to mellow her out and bring out the fun-loving side of her. I know Kris has a kind and loving heart. I think she is so often focused on business, her to do list, and the goals she has set for herself, that she pushes aside the softer elements of her personality.

When Bruce and Kris host parties for friends, I am invited to have a drink and join the party. These are some of my favorite moments, because I get to see the fun-loving Kris at her best.

Bruce and Kris often have a regular group of friends over for margaritas, chips, and a seven-layer guacamole dip that Kris makes. Their close friends include Kris's cousin (CeCe), Nicole Brown Simpson, Faye Resnick, Aisha, and two other friends, Ron and Joseph. I love it when they all come over, because there is always music playing and laughter in the air. Although it *is* my job to make sure that everyone has enough food and drink, I also get to hang out, have a margarita, and enjoy myself. Their friends treat me as if I was a part of the family, and during these parties, I never feel like the hired help.

Nicole Brown Simpson is one of Kris's closest friends, and they spend a great deal of time together. I like Nicole. She is straight and to the point — a strong personality that commands attention when she enters the room. She has a fun and carefree air about her. She is experiencing freedom from a difficult relationship after her divorce from O.J. Simpson. Nicole comes over often to hang out with Kris, who is trying to support her friend through her divorce, and to help out with her kids. Nicole and Kris have drinks together, laugh, and talk. Kris loosens up, smiles, and laughs. When Nicole is over, they are both so nice to me, laughing, joking around, offering me a drink, and treating me like a friend.

After working for Bruce and Kris for over a year, I have a few new items to add to my list of nanny rules:

MALIBU NANNY

1. Just do the things on my "to do" list and don't question them.

2. Agree with Kris.

3. Do not make excuses. They never work.

4. Always keep a few bottles of wine on hand.

CHAPTER EIGHTEEN
Trapezoids and Baby Tees

In my opinion, because of how I grew up in the Midwest, the kids seem spoiled in terms of material possessions. That doesn't mean they are naughty, but they do think they deserve the best of everything. Despite this, they are sweet, loving, well-behaved (for the most part — they *are* kids), and respectful children. Kris and Robert Kardashian have done a good job of parenting their children. Although they have everything they could ever want, they are *not* spoiled brats, which is actually surprising to me.

They are surrounded by wealth and affluence. The Hollywood scene and celebrities are a regular part of their lives. They've never known another way of living. Many of their friends are children of celebrities or celebrities themselves. Nicole Richie is a good friend of Kourtney and Kim. Other well-known friends of the kids include, Tatiana Ali (who plays the younger sister of Will Smith's character on the television show called *Fresh Prince of Bel Air*), Kimberly Stewart (Rod Stewart's daughter), Paris Hilton, and Justin and Sydney Simpson (OJ and Nicole's kids).

Justin and Sydney are best friends with Khloe and Robert. I shuttle the younger kids between our house and Nicole's house, usually every other day. Either the kids and me are over at Nicole's for a play date, or Sydney and Justin are at our house. Either way, I pick them up, drop them off, and babysit them. When Nicole comes over to hang out with Kris, she brings her kids along to play with Khloe and Robert. I get to know Sydney and Justin quite well. They are good kids, well behaved, and don't seem spoiled, despite their privileged upbringing.

Sometimes, as I look at the wealth and privilege around me, I long for the simple life in Minnesota. As I am fixing lunches for the kids one morning, I tell them about the Midwestern delicacies of lutefisk (a fish that smells incredibly strong and has an interesting jelly-like consistency), lefse (the Norwegian version of a tortilla, made with mashed potatoes), pickled herring (another fish dish that is preserved in a jar like dill pickles and usually eaten as an appetizer), and green jello "salad" made with shredded carrots and mayonnaise topping.

"Ewwww," they say in unison.

"Carrots and mayo in jello? That's disgusting," Kim adds, looking like she wants to throw up.

One night, I decide to make the family a Minnesota institution — the infamous "hotdish." Hotdish is a catch-all term that refers to an entrée made by combining random ingredients from your cupboard with a can of soup, and baking it for about an hour. Potato chips, tater tots, and mayonnaise are fairly common ingredients. I call my mom for the ingredients for my favorite tater tot hotdish, run to the store to grab tater tots (which are not an item Kris cares to keep stocked in the freezer), whip it together, and pop it in the oven.

Bruce and Kris are out of town. I wouldn't dare make it when they are around. So it's just the four kids and me for dinner. I plop a big scoop of the hotdish on each of their plates. They look at the meal on their plates and immediately begin to protest.

"This looks really weird."

"What's in it?"

"Gross. I'm not eating this."

"It looks like cat food or something."

"Okay, listen," I coax. "You have to at least try it. If you hate it, you don't have to eat it, but I think you will actually like it."

One by one, they each take the smallest bite possible on the end of their forks. As I suspect, they all like it, and finish their plates. Robert even asks for a second helping.

As I'm putting Robert to bed one night, we read a book about fishing. I tell him that I used to go ice fishing in Minnesota.

"What is ice fishing?" he asks.

"The lakes freeze in Minnesota, because it's so cold. And when the ice is thick enough, we cut a round hole in the ice, put a little house over it, and then drop a line and hook down into the water to catch fish."

"Wow, that's cool!" Robert exclaims. "I want to go ice fishing."

"Hopefully, I can take you some day," I respond, smoothing his hair, and planting a kiss on his forehead.

"Sweet dreams."

I lie in bed that night thinking of the countless hours I've spent fishing with my family back home. I doubt there are many people here in Malibu who would understand how ice fishing for seven or eight straight hours in a tiny four feet by four feet house in negative twenty-degree weather on a frozen lake could be classified as fun. I fall asleep with a smile on my face.

One day, Robert is eating a piece of candy, and he holds it out to me and says, "Look a trapezoid!"

With a puzzled look on my face, I respond, "What's a trapezoid?"

He comes up to me, grabs my arms and positions them parallel to each other and then places his two hands on the sides at an angle to make a sort of rectangular shape.

He beams up at me and says, "That's a trapezoid."

I go to the dictionary and look up "trapezoid" and sure enough, it says, "A four-sided flat shape with straight sides, that has a pair of opposite sides parallel." I roll my eyes and think, I really should have paid more attention in school. Now a five year old is teaching me new words.

The age gap between the older girls and the two younger kids is significant. Kourtney and Kim, who are into their teenage years (and all the drama and occasional attitudes that come along with it), are very close, while Robert and Khloe are buddies and share friends.

Kourtney and Kim hang out with the same group of friends and spend a lot of time together. They also have *huge* fights about clothes. They wear the same size, and literally on a daily basis, I hear them yelling at each other about an item of clothing.

"Those are my jeans! I just got them. Why are you wearing my jeans?" Kourtney screams at Kim.

"You stole my uniform! That was my shirt. Pam, she took my shirt out of my room," Kim yells the next day.

One of Kourtney's and Kim's favorite wardrobe items is the "baby tee" which seems to be popular with the teenage crowd. They are white, very tiny, skin-tight t-shirts that hug every curve. The girls buy child's sizes so it fits them snugly, and they are so tight that if one shrinks even slightly in the laundry, it won't fit them anymore. We buy package after package of white baby tees.

They *love* to shop, and Kourtney and Kim (like most teenage girls I'm sure) spend hour after hour in front of the mirror, trying on clothes, and picking out their outfits. Their favorite spots to shop are the Fred Segal store in Beverly Hills and the Beverly Center, a large upscale mall in West Los Angeles. They both have amazing fashion sense and always look cute and stylish. Kourtney loves high fashion, and wants to be a designer some day. She pours over fashion magazines and has many sketchbooks filled with her designs.

Shopping with their friends is one of their favorite activities. When they were pre-teen, I'd go with them to the mall. But as they have gotten older and more responsible, I drop Kim, Kourtney, and their friends at the mall to shop for a few hours or go to the movies.

The girls like to pick out clothes for me too, although I usually don't have the time or money to shop, but I do occasionally take their advice. One day when we are shopping at Fred Segal, they pick out a red and white polka dot Betsey Johnson sundress, which (even on sale) is more than I've ever paid for a dress before. Honestly, I buy it because they've suggested so many things to me that I've never been able to afford. I love it, however, and it becomes one of my favorite dresses.

Both Kourtney and Kim spend countless hours on the phone with their friends. I get really annoyed sometimes by their teenage attitudes. It's hard to tell them anything, because, of course, they know it all. If I had a penny for every time I've heard, "I know, Pam," I'd be wealthy.

Overall, they are good girls. We have never had any problems with drugs or alcohol. They don't sneak out, and I don't have any real disciplinary issues.

All four kids love their dad, Robert. They look forward to their weekends at his house. Robert Sr. is always friendly and appreciative towards me, and thanks me often for taking care of his kids.

One day as he brings them back to the house, he says, "Pam when the kids are at my house, all I hear is, Pam said this and Pam did that. I can tell how much they love you and how much time you spend with them." He continues, joking, "I'm so sick of hearing Pam, Pam, Pam."

Often when he calls the house to discuss pick up and drop off of the kids, he pretends to be someone else. With a really bad fake accent he says something like, "Hi Pam, this is Bobby. I met you last night at the bar. When can we go on a date?" It always puts a smile on my face.

Khloe loves her daddy so much, and when I drop the kids off on his weekends with them, Khloe is always the first one out the door, before the car even comes to a stop. Robert usually comes outside to greet us and kneels down to meet them. Khloe runs into his arms, and the other three join her. They all fall into a heap on the grass. It makes me smile. Robert loves his kids dearly, and they love him right back.

Occasionally, Robert has asked me to help out with the kids at his house, but that is rare. He doesn't have a nanny at his house. There is a housekeeper, but when the kids are with him, Robert spends quality time with them. He dearly loves each of his four children.

CHAPTER NINETEEN
Vamos a la Playa

As a nanny, I feel so fortunate to be able to travel — all expenses paid — usually in very luxurious accommodations. The only problem with the whole vacation idea is that it isn't *exactly* a vacation. It is a lot of work, but somehow I still always manage to have fun.

When school is out for the year, we take a vacation to a resort in Mexico with Nicole Brown Simpson, Sydney, and Justin. In addition to Bruce, Kris, the four kids, and myself, Burt and Casey join us.

We fly down in a private plane from Los Angeles. I'd always wanted to get off a private plane and wave as I was going down the steps, like I'd seen celebrities and dignitaries do so many times. So that's exactly what I do, and I have Kourtney pretend she is the paparazzi snapping pictures of me.

"You are such a nerd, Pam," she tells me, but does it anyway.

We stay at the very private La Costa Resort near Cabo San Lucas. Bruce and Kris have some friends that own a place down there — two beautiful, huge condos on a private beach.

The resort is a breathtaking paradise — endless white sand beaches that melt into the turquoise water under a cloudless azure sky, the calming sound of waves crashing on the shore, as palm trees dance in the gentle breeze.

The entire clan is out shopping one day, strolling around the bazaars and street vendors. I am admiring a sterling silver ring. Nicole notices, and says "Pam, I want to buy that for you." Despite my protest, she insists on getting it for me, which is a thoughtful gesture.

Another day, Nicole comes up to me, puts her hand on my shoulder, and says, "Pam, I don't know how you do it." I'm not exactly sure what she means, but I assume she is referring to watching all of the kids by myself. I single-handedly take care of Burt, Casey, Kourtney, Kim, Khloe, Robert, Sydney, and Justin, during the week long vacation. It is nice to have someone recognize and appreciate my effort.

Every day, the kids and I venture out into the cool, clear blue water about waist high with a handful of frozen peas. Jewel toned fish dart between our legs, so close we can touch them. We toss the frozen peas, and the fish quickly scoop them up. The kids scream in delight. I lose count of the number of bags of frozen peas I buy at the local market.

One thing I learn about Mexico is that it is a land of large insects. The adults are staying in one condo, and all of the kids and I sleep in the second condo. There aren't quite enough beds for everyone, so I am by myself on the couch in the living room area.

MALIBU NANNY

One night as I am sleeping, something bites my leg quite hard. I sit upright and brush it away. A huge, furry creature fills my entire hand. I jump up, as screams of terror escape my throat. I flip on the light, but can't find the culprit, which I assume is a monstrous spider. My screams wake all of the kids, who come running out of their bedrooms. I explain to them what happened. Kim and Kourtney are so freaked out that it takes them a long time to get back to sleep. The next day, they make me buy Raid, and Kourtney and Kim carry the cans of Raid around with them everywhere until we leave for home.

May 1992
Dear Dad & Mom,

Hi Honey bunnies! Well, it's our last night in Mexico and I'm feeling kinda sentimental. I just walked on the beach and the big dipper is so clear and distinct. Along with the hot weather, it reminded me of home on a hot summer night. We've had a great time. I've never killed so many insects and spiders in my life. Last night, a spider bit me so hard that it woke me and I felt it running down my leg so I brushed it away and it filled my whole hand. In other words, it was big! I also screamed pretty loud, but when I got up to turn on the light and look for it, it was gone, which made it rather hard for me to go back to sleep. I'm just going to stay awake all night tonight. Ha! Well, sorry about the crayon but I couldn't find a pen anywhere in the adult's condo, and hell if I'm going in the "spider" house!

I love you,
Pam

We take another vacation at the end of the year. In early December, we head to Whistler in British Columbia for a ski trip. Previously, I'd enjoyed British Columbia only during the summer cruises with David and Linda, so it's nice to see it during the winter season. Whistler is a beautiful, quaint city with cobbled streets and the old world charm of an alpine village. Covered in a layer of fresh white snow, with Christmas decorations everywhere, it feels like a winter wonderland.

Since I am in charge of the younger kids, I am also responsible for all of their ski gear. While Bruce and Kris are off skiing the slopes, and Kourtney and Kim are taking ski lessons and running around on their own in their very cute ski outfits from a ski shop in Beverly Hills, I get to "go skiing" with Robert and Khloe. Which means I spend a great deal of time watching them take lessons, schlepping them to the ski lift, and waiting for them at the bottom of the hills. I also haul around skis, boots, jackets, snow pants, hats, scarves, gloves, sleds, and other miscellaneous ski gear.

Despite the work, I *am* glad to be away from the usual routine, in a beautiful place, having a new experience. Yet, it's rather strange being in a gorgeous setting on a vacation but not sharing it with my friends or loved ones. I want to be happy, yet I feel an element of sadness, because I want more for my life than this. I am surrounded by my family of six, but, truthfully, I am lonely. It's not really *my* vacation.

To their credit, Bruce and Kris want me to have fun and spend some time exploring. They tell me, "Pam, you can go out when we get home."

But they are out until ten. Where am I going to go by myself at that time of night? I am not in the habit of bellying up to a bar solo for a drink.

Nevertheless, it is a fun vacation and a nice way to start the holiday season.

A few weeks later, I am back home in Minnesota for Christmas. My mom and I are in the kitchen one day making cookies as we listen to Christmas music on the radio. I hear a familiar melody, and recognize the lyrics immediately.

"Oh my gosh, Mom! This is 'Grown Up Christmas List'! I was there when it was written!" I exclaim.

I can't believe it. I sing along with the song, reminiscing about my amazing summer vacation in British Columbia with David, Linda, Brandon and Brody. I've been very lucky to go on some wonderful vacations — all expenses paid. Cruising in a yacht off the shore of British Columbia, skiing in Whistler, and enjoying a luxurious trip to Cabo San Lucas in Mexico — being a nanny definitely has its perks.

CHAPTER TWENTY
On My Own

In early 1993, Bruce and Kris sell their home in Malibu and move to a bigger house in Beverly Hills. Knowing that I am graduating soon and plan to find another job eventually, I take the opportunity to move out. I find an apartment in the Malibu Canyon Apartments complex (about twenty minutes straight east from Malibu) and room with two acquaintances from Pepperdine. I am a little short on money for my deposit, and I have no choice but to pull out the hundred-dollar bill from Erik Estrada that I have been saving for years. I kiss it goodbye, remembering what a highlight it was to meet him and talk with him.

Kris gives me a table and six chairs that she plans to replace with a new one. It is gorgeous high-end furniture. The table has a wood base that is carved to look like a tree trunk with birds sitting on the branches. It has a thick glass top. The chairs are hand carved wood as well, with a white fabric seat and back. Kris mentions that the table cost $10,000. I immediately think, that's an entire year of tuition for me. The table and chairs are elegant and look a bit out of place in my small apartment. Nevertheless, I am so appreciative to Kris for giving them to me.

Being a live-in nanny has become challenging, because I am *always* on the clock and the boundaries tend to be hazy. The kids would come to me at night if they had bad dreams or they were sick. And if I was home, even though it was technically my time off, I inevitably ended up working. Having my own place and being a live-out nanny/personal assistant makes a tremendous difference. I now have set hours and well-established boundaries. It is quite a concept — a fresh breath of air that gives me new focus.

Bruce and Kris buy a new Land Cruiser, which becomes my main mode of transportation. I'm more than happy to give up the old station wagon. I come to think of the Land Cruiser as "my car." Occasionally, Bruce needs to use it, but he always has to check with me first. Often, my answer is, "No I need it to pick up the kids," or, "No I need it to run an errand."

He teases me, replying, "Okay, well let me know when you are done with *your* Land Cruiser."

Since I am a broke college student, it is fun sometimes to pretend I have money —driving the BMW or Land Cruiser, shopping in Beverly Hills, and eating fine food. One day it is pouring rain, and I am driving the Land Cruiser, which needs to be filled up with gas. I do not want to get wet, but I have been instructed never to use the "full-service" side. Normally, I abide by this rule, but I really don't want to pump gas in the pouring rain. I'll do it this once, I tell myself. They'll never know. And, I pull into the full-service lane. While the attendant pumps gas in the rain, I touch up my makeup in the visor mirror, feeling quite important. As I flip up the visor and look over, there is Bruce standing next to his car, out in the rain, pumping his own gas. He glares at me, and wags his finger. I shrug with a sheepish grin on my face. It costs what — twenty cents more per gallon? An extra five bucks per tank of gas. That is nothing to them. But that is a no-no. Of course, I should have honored their rules. When we are both home later, before Bruce can say anything to me, I look at him and beg, "Bruce, *please* don't say a word. I'm sorry, and I won't do it again."

He doesn't say anything, but I can tell by the look on his face that I need to stay true to my word.

I make some new friends at Pepperdine. Two friends I meet through the music department, Heidi and Charity, talk me into joining them in a three-part harmony group. They need an alto to harmonize, and although voice is not my major, nor my strongpoint, I decide to take the risk since I am always looking for a new adventure. We get together weekly to practice, and decide to focus on music from the 1940's and 1950's, like "Boogie Woogie Bugle Boy" and "In the Mood."

After months of practice and a few minor gigs here and there, we hear that a nightclub called Tatoo in Beverly Hills is having auditions to hire a performance group for their dinner show. Knowing that Bruce and Kris frequent the place, I ask them to put in a good word for us, which they do. Name dropping works again. We get the gig.

Dressed in long black dresses, with our hair up and glamorous makeup, we play the part of classy mid-century songstresses. I thoroughly enjoy every moment of it, and allow myself to entertain (a little bit, at least) the newfound dream of a vocal career. We perform during the dinner hours at Tatoo, which turns into a dance club later in the evening. One night, I look out in the audience to see the cast of *90210* seated around a table.

Another night, my old flame, Sylvester Stallone, smiles back at me. He greets me with a hug after the show, and tells me I did a great job. It is nice to see him, and I feel the same magnetic pull, but our time together seems so long ago. My life has changed dramatically since we dated. It still seems surreal when I think about it. I actually dated a *mega* movie star. Yet, I knew him so well after spending countless hours on the phone. As a result, this chance meeting feels like a cordial exchange between old friends.

Unfortunately, my fledgling music career doesn't take off, as my two partners, for various personal reasons, choose not to continue performing, and our showbiz dreams fade abruptly.

CHAPTER TWENTY-ONE
Personal Shopper

Bruce loves to relax by watching TV, and whenever *The Nanny* (an eighties TV show starring Fran Drescher) is on, he calls down on the intercom and says, "Pam your show is on." The show makes a joke out of the bossy nanny who runs the household and their lives. When I watch it, I always think to myself, that truly is my reality.

I love my job, and I adore all four kids. I like being busy and shopping in Beverly Hills on a regular basis. Occasionally, I drive the BMW, which makes me feel really important. I have my own credit card, "Pam Behan for Bruce Jenner" inscribed on the front.

There are so many wonderful aspects to this job, and yet, I don't feel fulfilled. I have goals and dreams that I haven't pursued. I don't want to be a nanny forever. I am still living someone else's life. With my college graduation approaching soon, I begin to think about leaving.

The entire spring semester, I spend hours and hours preparing for my senior recital. I will be playing piano in front of my professors who will grade me on my performance. I must memorize seven songs. For two months, I practice two to three hours a day. Unfortunately, my mom and dad can't come to my recital, because they are planning to fly out for my upcoming graduation and they can't make both trips. I invite Kris, who promises to attend.

The night of the recital, before I leave the house to head to Pepperdine, Kim hands me a package.

"Here Pam, this is for you. I bought it with my own money," she says, beaming.

I am so surprised. I certainly didn't expect a gift.

"Thank you so much, Kim. That is so sweet of you."

I unwrap the brightly colored paper, and inside is a beautiful little ceramic and glass grand piano.

"Open it. It plays your favorite song," Kim quickly explains, before I can say anything.

I open the top of the piano, and the familiar notes of "Music Box Dancer" begin to play.

"Oh my gosh. Kim, I can't believe you bought this for me. Wow. This means so much to me," I say to her, with tears in my eyes.

Kim smiles shyly. I am quite shocked. It is a beautiful, thoughtful, meaningful gift from a teenager.

The night of my senior recital, I'm so happy to see Kris there. My friend Anne also shows up. One of my pieces is the tune from the music box Kim gave me — "Music Box Dancer." I've been playing it since I was a little girl. Before I begin the piece, I dedicate it to my mom. I happen to glance over at Kris as I play, and I see tears in her eyes. It means so much that she is there, and I'm touched that she is emotional about by my performance.

That night, as I lie in bed, I reflect on the day. I saw a tender and loving side of Kris today, and it really affected me. I think about how, just a few months ago, she wrote my tuition check to Pepperdine for the spring semester. I didn't have enough cash, and I was so nervous to ask her, but she was happy and willing to help. I had to work it off, of course, but it was still a kind and generous gesture, not to mention trusting (that I would stick around to pay it off).

Despite my frustrations with the Kris who has high expectations and little praise, I must always remember this warm and thoughtful side of her as well.

In April, I graduate from Pepperdine University with a Bachelors of Arts degree in Piano and Trumpet Performance. I'm thankful my parents and brother get to witness me receiving my degree. It is a huge sense of accomplishment. Not only

did I pay my way through college, but I worked my butt off for four years, kept up a full load of courses, and graduated on schedule.

Now that I have my degree, I plan to move on and pursue a new career. After avoiding the issue for some time, I finally mention my idea to Kris one day. I plan the moment carefully, approaching her when she seems relaxed, and has a glass of wine in her hand. I figure it might improve my chances of a positive response.

"Kris, I've been meaning to talk to you about something," I begin — nervous about how she will react.

"Oh, what's that Sweetie?" she replies, turning her full attention to me.

"Well, I've been working here for two years, and you know my plan all along was to start pursuing a career once I graduated," I take a breath and continue, "I really feel like I need to start looking for another job."

"Oh, Pam, why on earth would you want to leave?" Kris says, astonishment registering on her face. "Please don't leave now. It would be so hard to replace you."

"But, I promised myself I'd pursue a career once I graduated, Kris," I explain. "I don't want to be a nanny forever."

"Of course, I know that. But just stay for a while," she pleads. "And when you do leave, Bruce and I will help you find a great job. It will be no problem. We know *everyone*."

I think it was the significant emphasis on "everyone" that made me stay.

Now that I have no college classes during the day and all four kids are in school, my job duties change somewhat. Personal assistant to Kris becomes my primary role and responsibility. The change in roles is nice. Maybe I can do this for a while longer.

Had we signed a contract when I accepted the new role of Personal Assistant to Kris, I imagine the wording might have gone something like this:

You shall function as my personal assistant and shall perform a list of duties, subject to change, at my full discretion, at any time. Such duties must be performed immediately and as efficiently and quickly as possible, and may include, but are not limited to, any or all of the following activities: appointment scheduler, answering service, delivery person, errand runner (errands include, but are not limited to, the following: grocery shopping, personal shopping, birthday shopping, clothes shopping, any and all other shopping deemed necessary, dry cleaning, returns, etc.) chauffer to children, car washer, counselor, cook, household manager, etc., et al, ad nauseum.

The shopping part of the job is the most fun. I get to drive the Land Cruiser or BMW, hang out in Beverly Hills, on Sunset Boulevard (an exclusive shopping area in West Los Angeles) or the Beverly Center, and shop all day. I am living the life of the rich and famous, even though I am neither rich nor famous.

One of my regular destinations is a jewelry store in Beverly Hills called 14 Carat. Kris likes to purchase high-end jewelry for her friends and family, so I shop there often for birthday and Christmas gifts. When I walk through the door, they know me well, and are eager to assist because they know I will always be spending money. It always makes me think of the scene in *Pretty Woman* when Vivian takes Edward's credit card and goes shopping on Rodeo Drive, and the clerks all bustle about serving her.

One day, I step into the elevator in the store (it is two floors), and turn around. Richard Simmons steps in and stands right next to me. He is dressed in his usual workout attire — tank top and shorts — and curly afro.

"Hi Richard," I say, hoping he's friendly to strangers.

"Hello! How are you?" Richard responds, as peppy and perky as you would expect him to be.

"I'm great." We've reached the bottom floor and the doors are opening, so I say, "Have a great day!"

"Oh you too, sweetie," he responds, turning around to smile.

Running into celebrities has become a weekly occurrence. I realized a long time ago that they are just people. There are occasions, however, when I still am very excited to meet a star that I used to idolize. *Charlie's Angels* was one of my favorite shows, and I wanted to be just like the Angels. I have seen Farrah Fawcett numerous times in Malibu. I also run into Jaclyn Smith regularly, because her kids go to the same high school as Kourtney and Kim. And recently, I rode in a limousine with Cheryl Ladd. It's quite amazing that I've met all three Angels.

It's nice having Bruce's credit card with my name on it. I feel important when I sign my name. It is fun shopping with someone else's money. Sometimes when I look at the totals on my purchases, I am in shock.

Often Kris will have an idea of what she wants, and she asks me to purchase two or three different options. I bring them home, she chooses which one she wants, and I return the rest. So I make many trips to return unused items.

Once a week, I stop at Starbucks to pick up a bag of coffee beans. Kris tells me to get myself a coffee drink. Other than that, I never use the card for any personal items. I would never think about abusing the privilege. I buy gas to fill the cars and make purchases for Bruce and Kris. If I am buying things for the kids like ice cream or food, Kris gives me cash for that.

Being a personal assistant for Kris keeps me incredibly busy. Shopping all the time is fun for a while, but eventually I start to tire of it, and realize again that I need to get focused on my career. If only I knew what I wanted to do with my life.

CHAPTER TWENTY-TWO
Sleazy Hotel

It has been months since my musical group disbanded. I get a call in mid-summer from a music producer named Lonny in Ontario, California (whom we had been referred to by a friend). We met him once, and made plans to make a demo tape, but never made it past the planning stage.

"Pamela, are you and your friends ready to record an album?" he inquires.

"Oh, Lonny, I'm sorry, but we aren't a group anymore. My friends dropped out for personal reasons," I tell him.

"Too bad for them. But you don't need them. You can do it on your own. Go solo as a country artist. I'll help you," Lonny responds enthusiastically.

"I don't know, Lonny. I'm not that talented," I reply dismissively.

"Pamela, you've got it all! The looks. The voice. The moves. You are going to be big!" Lonny exclaims, talking faster and louder. "I have this song I've been trying to promote for ten years. I've always said, 'Lonny, when you find the right person this song is going to be huge.' I think YOU are the right person, Pam!"

"Really? You think I've got what it takes?" I am still skeptical, but Lonny seems *so* excited. "What is the name of the song?"

"I want to spend the night in a sleazy hotel with you."

I burst out laughing.

"Lonny, you have got to be kidding me," I say, trying to stifle my laugh. "I can't sing that."

"I know it sounds a little funny but think of some of the biggest country hits over the years," Lonny says, pausing. I can tell he's taking a drag on a cigarette. He continues, "Many of them have off the wall titles, like 'It wasn't

God who Made Honky Tonk Angels' and 'Don't Come Home a Drinkin.' Trust me, it's going to be huge!"

I hadn't heard of either of those songs, and I am not convinced.

"Gosh, I don't know, Lonny. I don't think I can sing that. It sounds so… well…sleazy," I reply.

"But wait, Pamela. I haven't told you about the video," Lonny says with excitement.

He goes on to explain his concept for the music video for this supposed huge country hit. A bride and groom who have just married are driving in a convertible. They are on a back road, driving through the desert on their way home from Las Vegas. They come across a run down sleazy motel out in the middle of nowhere. There is nothing around for miles. The bride sings to her husband, "I want to spend the night in a sleazy motel with you."

Hearing the concept for the video makes the song a bit more palatable, since the couple is married. What else do I have going for me right now? I have a degree in music. Maybe this is what I am supposed to be doing. What do I have to lose? I may as well give it a shot. Take a risk and go for it.

"Well, okay, Lonny, I'll give it a try," I reply.

"Great! That's just great, Pamela. It is going to be huge! You are going to be a big star!"

A couple weeks later, I drive to his place in Ontario. I knock on a door at the back of the house, as instructed. Lonny opens the door and invites me into his one-room studio. The room is small and smells strongly of cigarette smoke. The walls are covered with wood paneling, and faded black velvet drapes cover the two windows. On one side of the room is an old desk with a green leather chair behind it. The other half of the room is filled with recording equipment and a keyboard.

Lonny, who is about six foot one, and looks to be around sixty years old, is clad in a pale green button up shirt, and khaki pants. I am comforted by the fact that he looks somewhat professional. I think I'd be more concerned if he was wearing polyester and gold chains. He lights a cigarette, inhales deeply, and peers at me.

"Are you ready to get started, Pamela?"

He mailed me the lyrics and sheet music for the song, so I've been practicing for about a week. Lonny asks me to sing through the song one time so he can see how I do. He shows me where to stand, and then pushes a button on the panel. The instrumental notes of the song fill the room.

"Do you know where to jump in?" he yells over the music.

"Yes," I yell back.

I feel the performance goes fairly well. Lonny, who has been leaning back in the green leather chair throughout the song, stands up and walks slowly over to me.

"Pamela," he says, shaking his head. "We have some work to do."

I am in the studio for about two hours. Line by line, Lonny shows me exactly how he wants me to perform the song — inflections, tone, volume, facial expressions, hand gestures, hip gyrations, and movement around the "stage."

"Pamela, you need to loosen up," he says at one point. "You look too nervous and stiff."

Watching Lonny shake his hips like a woman and throw his imaginary long hair back is comical. I wonder to myself if this is how most record producers operate.

I do my best to shake it like Lonny.

"Pamela, make your voice more raspy in this section," he instructs, and repeats a line in a throaty female impersonation, which sounds really horrible.

I'm channeling Tina Turner performing "What's Love Got to Do With It" as I sing the section over again, hoping it doesn't sound anything like he just did.

A week later, I return for more intensive instruction from my "vocal coach." After two hours, he either thinks I'm actually ready to perform or he's given up on improving me, and announces, "Okay, Pamela. I want you to audition for my partner in Las Vegas."

Lonny has a business partner named Albert who will have the final say. If he likes me, Albert will find a third party who will produce the record and a music video. I was under the initial impression that Lonny would produce the record, but I guess he is more of a talent scout. And vocal coach of course. This music business is complicated. I had no idea there were so many steps in the process.

I'm a little leery of the whole thing, since I am supposed to meet Albert in a hotel room at the Aladdin in Vegas. I can be really naive, but even *I* know bad things can happen to a girl in Vegas. I talk Smitty into going with me.

After a five-hour drive, we pull up to the Aladdin in my Thunderbird. We step into the lobby and recognize Albert immediately, because Lonny instructed, "Just look for the huge guy with black glasses." Albert, who has a buzz cut and dark black rimmed glasses, is about six feet, three inches tall and must be close to three hundred pounds. He is wearing a yellow button up polyester shirt and polyester pants with a belt. I'm glad I'm wearing sunglasses, because the buttons on the shirt look like they are about to pop off at any moment. I notice a gold chain around his neck. Uh oh. Polyester and gold chains. Big red flag.

Albert announces he is taking us to lunch first and leads us out to his convertible Cadillac. Smitty climbs in the back, and I sit in the front. As we drive to the restaurant, I keep sneaking sideways glances at Smitty, who has her hands over her mouth the entire ride. I hear snorts and giggles. I try so hard not to laugh, but I am on the verge of losing it. I pinch my arm to distract myself. I doubt any major country music star got their start this way. I'm thankful I brought Smitty with me.

After lunch, we head back to the Aladdin and take the elevator to Albert's room. I have dressed up for my audition. I am wearing a white sheer blouse, a white flowing skirt with a colorful flower motif, and white high heels.

"So where do you want me?" I ask Albert, and bite my lip, as I realize I might not want to be saying that.

"Oh just stand over there by the window," he responds. "Smitty, you can sit on that chair in the corner."

Albert plops himself down on the edge of the king size bed, and the whole bed shakes and groans.

I pull my cassette tape player out of my bag, pop in the cassette with the background music on it, and push the play button.

I am nervous, sweating, and have to pee. I glance at Smitty, who has her head buried in her knees. I can see her shaking, so I know she is laughing. I am going to kill her.

I focus on Albert and dive into the song. As I sing, "I Want to Spend the Night in a Sleazy Motel with You," I think the song choice couldn't be any more inappropriate for this moment.

Despite the distraction in the corner and the crazy thoughts bouncing around my head, I think I perform the song fairly well. Albert doesn't say much.

"Sing it again please."

I repeat my performance, avoiding even a glance at Smitty. I'm glad I can't hear her above the music. I assume she's still laughing.

"That was good. Very good, Pam," Albert announces. "Thank you for coming to audition. I will be in touch. I need to make a few calls to my associates, and we'll try to get you hooked up with someone who can produce your record."

Smitty and I both shake Albert's hand. As we walk through the door, I smack her in the back of the head. The moment the door closes, we both dissolve into cackling laughter. I grab her hand and pull her down the hall so Albert can't hear us.

What a joke.

"What was that?" I ask, between fits of laughter.

"I have no idea, but I sure am glad I came with you," she responds, doubling over again, as tears run down her face.

So much for my recording career.

CHAPTER TWENTY-THREE
Nicole and O.J.

My birthday rolls around again. I am twenty-five years old. It's hard to believe I was only nineteen when I moved to California to be a nanny for the summer. Six years have passed already. I never would have guessed that I'd still be working as a nanny. I want to do something else with my life, but I don't know what. I spent a lot of money to get a degree in music. I should probably be pursuing music. But, I tried a recording career, and it didn't work out so well. Maybe it's a sign from God.

For my birthday, Kris gives me a beautiful ceramic pitcher and bowl. I place it in the middle of the glass table they gave me when I moved in. For a young woman with a small apartment, I have some high end furnishings.

In the early part of 1994, I am working at Gladstones one day and overhear two women talking about their singing group. After telling me a little about their history, Deb and Mimi offer to let me audition. Despite my disastrous Vegas foray into the music industry, I'm willing to give it another shot. God may have been trying to tell me something, but I'm choosing not to listen. I need a new career desperately.

We meet a week later; I sing for them; and we agree to form a trio. Since the 1940's and 1950's music style worked fairly well for my previous group, we decide to focus on the same songs. After practicing for a few weeks, we land a gig to perform at a Veteran's banquet at a hotel. We also audition for a Snapple commercial, singing a song with three-part harmony that we wrote ourselves. To our surprise, we don't get a callback.

On June 13, 1994, I am practicing with my new group. The television happens to be on in the background. A newscaster announces that Nicole

148

Brown Simpson has been found dead, the apparent victim of a homicide. I am in shock. I know this woman and her kids so well. I was with her just days ago. I've never had anyone close to me die in a tragedy. I feel so helpless. I question God. Why would He allow this to happen? Life is suddenly incredibly fragile.

The three of us sit and watch television for hours, as my stomach churns. I am heartbroken for her children, and for Khloe and Robert. How will this be explained to them, and what will it do to their little hearts?

Within days, O.J.'s name starts to swirl as a suspect. I met him only once, briefly, at a hotel. Bruce had a speaking engagement at a hotel, and I was there to pick him up. O.J. came over to the car, and said hi. That's the only interaction I ever had with him.

I knew from previous conversations with Kris and Nicole that Robert and Kris started dating about the same time that Nicole and O.J. met. O.J. and Robert were best friends, and so the two couples started to spend a great deal of time together, and Nicole and Kris became dear friends. Nicole filed for divorce not long after I began working for Bruce and Kris.

A couple of weeks after Nicole was killed (with O.J. now in jail as a suspect), I bring Khloe and Robert to visit Sydney and Justin at Nicole's parents house in Laguna Beach. Khloe, Robert, and I stay for a few days and hang out with Sydney and Justin to give them some sense of normalcy. One day, I even take them to a water park, which is scary for me, because there are threats to kidnap the Simpson kids. I try to push it out of my mind and focus on doing what I can to help Sydney and Justin cope with what is happening to them.

All sense of a normal life was swept away the day their mother was killed, and their father put in jail for suspected murder. Sydney and Justin had played with Khloe and Robert all the time. Suddenly, they were taken away from their home, their friends, and their normal schedule of daily life. I bring the kids over several times for play dates to help them forget about the craziness swirling around them.

It is a horribly sad and tragic event that happened to people I knew and saw regularly. It impacts everyone, and our household is shaken. We all walk around in a fog for a while. All of the kids, but especially Khloe and Robert, are in shock. They ask *why* did it happen? How do you answer a question like that?

All I can say is, "I don't know, honey. I don't know."

They are very disturbed and have many questions. They wake up in the middle of the night with bad dreams and more questions. They just keep asking, "Why?"

Robert Kardashian stands by his best friend O.J. and becomes a volunteer member of the legal team. As the pre-trial publicity swirls, jury selections are made, and the legal teams are introduced to the public, the "Kardashian" name is suddenly everywhere. It is surreal.

Although the divorce created a divide between Robert and Kris, they have been fairly civil and friendly with each other over the years. Robert's choice to defend O.J. creates a chasm of incredible tension between them. I'm sure Kris is not surprised, since Robert and O.J. are best friends, but she is loyal to Nicole and her kids, and she can't hide her resentment about this role he's chosen to take on. It is extremely awkward, and I am caught in the middle. Of course, the trial takes up most of Robert's time, so he doesn't spend much time with the kids. When I do see him, he is not his normal, jovial self.

The entire family is in turmoil. It is a difficult time to be a nanny in this home.

CHAPTER TWENTY-FOUR
A Bun in the Oven

I fly home for a week over the holidays. Everyone is in disbelief about the murder and trial, and they have so many questions. What did I see? What did I know? I came back home hoping to escape the craziness, but it has followed me.

When I return from Minnesota, a friend of mine asks me to help him move on New Year's Day. I am loyal to my friendship with him and call in to Gladstones to tell them I can't work that day. Gladstones has a policy that major holidays are mandatory attendance, and they caution me that I could be fired.

I take the day off anyway, and unfortunately, they fire me to make an example out of me and stick by their policy.

January 13, 1995
Dear Dad & Mom,

Good morning! How are you doing? I'm doing fine, despite losing my job. ☺

Bruce & Kris have been very nice to me and said they'd help me in any way possible. For now that means paying me to work for them. Today was my first day off in about three weeks. I don't mind that I've been working so much but I must admit that it was very nice to have the day off.

I'm having fun with the kids here. Kourtney has improved a lot with her driving and she loves to take her nanny Pam for rides. Ha! Kim has a boyfriend who is so nice and polite. He's really shaped Kim up too. Khloe has really grown and Robert is my little angel. He cried after his haircut today. You two meadow muffins take care!

All my love,
Pam

XXXOOO

PS – Bruce and Kris say Hi!

As the Simpson trial is just getting underway in early 1995, I have an unusual dream one night. In the dream, Kris is pregnant, goes into labor, and gives birth to a baby. I go to the hospital to visit, but a security guard stands at the door, telling me I can't go into her room. Bruce and Kris hear my voice and call out to the guard that it is okay to let me in, because I am family.

When I wake up the next morning, I recall the dream. I wonder about its meaning. I guess there is a strong desire for me to be treated like family. I love the kids, and I treat them as if they are my own, and it would be nice to know that they (and Bruce and Kris) feel the same way. I miss my own family back home, and I do have a strong desire for my own husband and kids someday. I suppose I am craving that family connection, and it is showing up subconsciously in my dreams.

Later that morning, as Kris is giving me her "to do" list for the day, I tell her about the dream. She looks at me funny but doesn't say anything. That night, when I bring the kids home from school, Bruce and Kris call them up to their room for a family meeting. A short while later, the kids come down the stairs. Khloe and Robert are yelling, "Mom's having a baby! Mom's having a baby!"

Kris has a huge smile on her face, as she looks at me.

"I can't believe it! I dreamed you were pregnant!"

"I know," she says. "I wanted to tell you so badly this morning, but I had to wait until I told the kids first."

Bruce and Kris (who is now thirty-nine) have been trying to get pregnant for a long time, so they are overjoyed at the news.

As the trial progresses, so does Kris's pregnancy. Although I'm thrilled for Bruce and Kris, and excited to meet the baby, the pregnancy hastens my desire to move on. I am increasingly frustrated with life in Los Angeles. It has been two years since I graduated from Pepperdine, and I am still working at this nanny job. I know that if I spend much time with the baby and bond with him or her, I will have a hard time leaving. I don't want to look up one day and realize another four or five years have passed. I'm adamant that I will not allow that to happen. It is time to spread my wings and make a life for myself outside of the lives of the Jenner and Kardashian families.

I begin taking tennis lessons, at Smitty's insistence, to get my mind off of my career dilemma. I am horrible and can't get the hang of it. One day after a particularly bad lesson, the Pepperdine tennis coach, Gualberto, pulls me aside and says, "Pam, what do you want to do with your life?"

Ever the jokester, I casually flip the tennis racket upside down and with head banging, hair flying, and wild "air guitar" strums, I yell, "I want to be a rocker!"

"Well, that's good, Pam," Gualberto says, as serious as can be. "I'm just happy you didn't say tennis, because you really stink at tennis."

It makes me realize I need to take stock of my life and figure out, what *do* I want to do with my life? I know I don't want to be a nanny forever. I've been thinking about quitting for a long time.

I planned to find another job after I graduated, but Kris talked me out of it. Now, two more years have come and gone. I want to leave. I think about it all of the time, but I don't know where I will go or what I will do. I have no clearly defined career aspirations at the moment. Do I move back to the Midwest, try a completely different part of the country, or stay in California? I've finally realized vocal performance is not my true calling. I return to my dream of being a cruise director. I still have a desire to explore and see the world.

Candace Garvey used to be a flight attendant, and she has a friend who might be able to get me a job on a private plane. Maybe I should attempt to be a flight attendant. Questions float through my brain mercilessly with no clear answers.

So I wait. I continue working for Kris and taking care of the kids, because I don't know what else to do.

CHAPTER TWENTY-FIVE
Drooling, Driving, and Dating

Khloe has a special fondness for animals, especially horses and dogs. She wants to be a veterinarian when she grows up. She gives most of her attention to the dog, Harley. One of the firm rules I have for Harley is no table food. Khloe doesn't like my rule, and often tries to sneak food to Harley. One night, we have bow tie pasta for dinner. After the kids leave the table, I am in the kitchen cleaning up. Harley throws up — a nice little pile of bow tie pasta. I call to Khloe in the next room.

"Khloe, did you feed Harley from the table again?"

She yells back, "No!"

To which I respond, "Really? Well, can you come here for a moment?"

I show her the small mound of perfectly formed bow tie pasta on the floor. A sheepish smile covers her face. Without saying anything, I hand her a paper towel to clean it up. She disappears for a moment and comes back with a bandana covering her nose and mouth. With exclamations of "yuck" and "ewww," she cleans up the mess.

After years of begging Bruce and Kris, Khloe starts taking horseback riding lessons. I am happy to take her, because I love horses too.

Khloe is unhappy that I am single and considers it her mission to match me up with someone…anyone. She is constantly trying to set me up with *any* man she thinks is single and available, as long as they are somewhat within my

age range. Most of the men she suggests to me are too old, too young, or not my type.

I am not surprised when, after the first couple of riding lessons, she starts telling me about her instructor Dan.

"Pam, he is so cute," she gushes. "I really think you should date him."

Based on my past experiences with her, I don't give much thought to it.

One day, as we drive up to the riding ring for her lesson, I see a young man around my age riding a horse, and he is ruggedly handsome, in a Marlboro Man sort of way.

I say, "Khloe is *that* your riding instructor?"

She looks at me with excitement in her eyes and exclaims, "Yes! You like him, don't you?!"

Without another word, she jumps out of the Land Cruiser and runs towards Dan, yelling. "My nanny likes you! My nanny likes you!"

As I get out of the car, she tells him to come over and meet me. I watch as he rides toward me (in slow motion, it seems). He is dressed in chaps, boots, and cowboy hat. His horse's mane and tail flow in the wind. It is like a scene from a movie. I can't believe Khloe is introducing this hunky man to me.

Dan is friendly as can be, but, unfortunately, nothing ever happens between us. During the hour she has her lesson each week, I wait there with Khloe, admiring from afar the Marlboro Man.

Kourtney will be sixteen soon, and she needs to learn how to drive. It naturally falls to me to teach her how to drive. Lucky me. That girl just can't get the hang of it. She steps on the gas pedal when she should be hitting the brake, and she stomps fiercely on the brake when she should be accelerating.

One day as we are driving, she almost drives off the road. The window is open, and as I yell at her to turn, I look to the right, straight into a blur of bright pink flowers and green leaves. She is so far off the road that we nearly take out a huge bush.

Thankfully, by the time her birthday arrives, she has mastered driving. I'm glad we both survive those driving lessons without injury.

For her sweet sixteen birthday, Kourtney gets a brand new black BMW from Bruce and Kris. The entire family goes out to dinner, and Bruce and Kris have the car delivered to the restaurant. I am thrilled for Kourtney, but surprised by the gift. How many sixteen year olds get a brand new BMW?

Kourtney and Kim (who is now fourteen) like hanging out with their close-knit group of friends. One weekend, Robert Kardashian is out of town, and he asks me to watch the kids at his house. Kourtney and her boyfriend, Jeff (who is an extremely good looking boy), have a few friends over.

Jeff is a good kid. He is tan, athletic, outgoing, and personable. He has me wrapped around his pinkie. I tell Kourtney often, even in front of him, "Wow your boyfriend is cute!" Whenever they want to do something together or they need me to drive them somewhere, she tells Jeff to ask me, because I'm more likely to say yes.

On the night in question, I ask Jeff, Kourtney, and their friends to hang out in the main rooms of the house and stay out of the bedrooms. I head upstairs to hang out with Khloe and Robert, and give Kourtney and her friends some privacy. When I check on them later, Kourtney and Jeff are in her dad's bedroom alone. I knock on the door once or twice. She opens the door right away.

"Kourtney, I asked you to stay out of the bedroom. Please come out."

"Pam, we're not doing anything!"

The girls are pushing for independence. I understand their need for excitement and more freedom. It was only a few years ago I was their age. I try to cut them some slack, and bend the rules at times when it's not a critical issue. Nevertheless, I make them come out to the living room.

With Kourtney and Kim, I often feel like I am trying to win their approval. When they were a little younger I mostly ignored their pre-teen attitudes, but as they get older (and seem closer to me in age), I want them to like me. I have grown to love them, and I want them to love me back. I guess that is a lot to ask, because I am their nanny, aka, rule maker, party-ruiner, and fun spoiler. Friend is probably not on the list of names they (or their friends) have for me. Deep down, I know they love me, even if I never hear those words from them.

One of the boys in the group decides to go home, and walks out the front door, setting off the security alarm. Since this is Robert's house, I have no idea how to turn off the alarm, and the girls can't figure it out either. The house is filled with an extremely loud, blaring, "Waaap. Waaap. Waaap." Over and over. We can't get the darn thing to stop. The phone rings. Who on earth is calling the house at two a.m.?

"Hello, Ma'am, this is the security company. Is there an emergency at your home? Do you need us to send a car out?"

"Uh, no. I am the nanny," I explain, sheepishly. "There is no emergency. We just accidentally set off the alarm by opening the door. We're fine."

"Okay, Ma'am. No problem."

"Umm, but could you help me out? We can't figure out how to turn off the alarm." I say, flustered and embarrassed.

"Oh. Okay. No problem. We can reset it from here."

It is two in the morning, the alarm is still blaring, the rap music is blasting from the other room, and I am done.

"Okay, party is over!" I yell.

Kourtney and Kim have a few other parties when Bruce and Kris are out of town. By "parties," I mean a small group of friends, rap music (playing loud), snacks, and sodas. I usually kick their friends out around two or three in the morning, mainly because I have to get up early the next morning, and I need my sleep. I know Kourtney and Kim don't drink during the parties they have at the house. I know because I check. I smell their breath, and I check the garbage cans inside and the trash bins outside. It is possible their friends snuck liquor of some kind in or out, but I never catch anyone. We have never had any problem with alcohol, drugs or smoking. And for that, I am grateful.

All four kids love Michael Jackson, but especially Kim. She and I spend many hours in her bedroom, practicing the moves to Michael Jackson's *Thriller* and from the movie *Flashdance* on her floor.

Kim starts dating T.J. Jackson, who is Michael Jackson's nephew. T.J. and his brothers are in a popular R&B boy band called 3T. He is a handsome young man, very polite, and rather quiet. He comes over to the house often to hang out with Kim. They get serious quickly and become an exclusive couple.

They spend a lot of time together. After school, they do homework together and watch television or movies. Most of their dates are just hanging out at our house, but occasionally they go to the mall for shopping or a movie, or out to eat.

Oh the beauty and sweetness of young love. Kim and T.J. are best friends and seem to have a close and caring relationship. I understand why she fell for him. He treats her with great respect. He is rather quiet, but genuinely nice and kind.

Kim's personality is on the quiet side too. She is introspective and keeps to herself, but she is a sweet girl. Given her beauty, I almost expect her to be self-centered or egotistical. Kim has always been gorgeous. I catch myself sometimes staring at her natural beauty. Of course, she knows she is beautiful, because everyone always tells her she is beautiful. Yet, she maintains her sweetness. I'm glad she hasn't allowed her beauty to go to her head.

One day, we are on our way to Culver City after school for Khloe's ice skating lesson. The other three kids have to go along for the ride, and they're not that happy about it. With L.A. traffic, everything takes so long, and they are tired. The noise level in the car keeps increasing, and despite my repeated requests for them to quiet down, there is a lot of whining and yelling going on.

I've had enough. I change lanes and pull the car over into the emergency lane on the right side of the road, stop the car, and turn on the emergency flashing lights.

"You guys won't listen to me. So I'm going to sit here now until the police arrive."

I wasn't serious but wanted to get their attention so they would listen to me and quiet down.

Robert starts crying, and pleads, "I'll be good. I'll be good. Please don't wait for the police."

"Okay," I say. "But, no more talking and yelling."

I pull back into traffic, and the rest of the trip is extremely peaceful and quiet.

Occasionally, I have Khloe and Robert over to my apartment to spend the night. When I'm getting ready to head home after working at their house all day, they beg me to let them come over. I'm not getting paid for this time, but I just can't say no to them.

May 7, 1995
Dear Dad & Mom,

I'm babysitting right now. I have been with Khloe and Robert since Friday at noon. They stayed with me at my apartment Friday night, and then Saturday morning, we all (Bruce and Kris too) went to Disneyland and stayed the night. Bruce had to make an appearance for some fitness program. Arnold Schwarzenegger was there too. Then we had a tour guide walk us around the park so we didn't have to wait in lines. I thought of "our" trip to Disneyland. That first time with you was the absolute best. Well, I'll talk to you real soon.

All my love,
Pam

CHAPTER TWENTY-SIX
Leaving "The Hills"

I continue to mention to Kris now and then my interest in finding a career. True to her word, she sets up an interview with her cousin CeCe, who owns a literary agency in Beverly Hills. CeCe is looking for a "literary assistant," which is quite funny considering I don't like to read or write. We actually get to the point of discussing the hours I will work, but then Kris talks me out of it.

"What did she say she would pay you? I'll match it. That's not what you really want to do anyway. Just stick with us here for now. We'll find you something great eventually."

Again, I stay.

By now, every fiber of my being tells me it is time to go. My dream from high school of traveling and seeking great adventure lives on. I want to explore and see other parts of the country and the world besides the Midwest and California. I've switched my focus from cruise director to flight attendant, thinking I'll have more freedom to have a social life if I'm not marooned on a boat all of the time.

In the summer of 1995, I send applications to several airlines, attend open houses, and follow up on any and all connections to the airlines that I happen to come across.

While I am pursuing a career with the airlines, I am also contemplating a completely different venture. The father of my good friend, Kirk, asks me to move to Tennessee to manage a convenience store (a brand new store that he is building). The store manager salary is twice what the airlines would pay me as a flight attendant, and I would also receive some stock ownership.

Because I am nearing that critical age when women start hearing the tick of the clock, there is a part of me that wants to settle down in one place and start focusing on marriage and children. I am ready for a significant change and moving from California to the South would be revolutionary. There's also the draw of the country life. Because of my love for horses as a child, I've always dreamed about living on a horse farm in Kentucky some day. Tennessee is right next door. Can't be too much different from Kentucky. I spent time in Tennessee when Linda was filming "Hee Haw," and I really loved it. I conclude that it would be fun to move to a completely new and different part of United States and start to give *serious* consideration to moving down South.

I fly to Tennessee to meet with my friend's father, look at the building site, and discuss details. The trip goes well, and, although I haven't made a decision, I find I am leaning towards Tennessee.

June 15, 1995
Dear Dad & Mom,

Hello there! How are you doing? Good, I hope. Everything is going real well for me lately. Ever since I got back from Tennessee, Kris has been an angel. I think she realized while I was away how much I do for her. A mom of one of Robert's friends asked me if I could work for her when I'm not at the Jenner's. I think that's why Kris has been so nice to me lately.

The Airlines: American is now hiring and I met an American flight attendant who said she'd give me a recommendation, so I'm applying. And the other day, Candace Garvey (Steve Garvey's wife) came up to me and said she's got a job for me, as a flight attendant for their friend's private airplane. I'll keep you updated.

Love you,
Pam

After the lengthy O.J. Simpson trial, which I follow occasionally, I watch television, along with millions of Americans, on October 3, 1995, as the verdict is read. Not guilty. I am in shock once again. I truly believe he is guilty, and I am sick to my stomach. It is hard for everyone in the family, and it opens fresh wounds.

The combination of Kris being pregnant and the not guilty verdict are the final straws in a haystack that is about to tip over. I give Bruce and Kris my notice a few days later. It is time to move on.

Nicole's death was traumatic for me. But now, the person who ended her life (in my opinion) isn't being held accountable for his actions. It is devastating for me. I have an overwhelming feeling about the sanctity of life and how short it is. Nicole's life ended so tragically and so early. Yet here I am, not progressing, and not making the most of the life I do have. I can't do it anymore.

I still haven't made a final decision about whether to head to Tennessee or accept a flight attendant position, but giving my notice will force me to make a choice, and put a time frame on my departure. I tell Bruce and Kris I will be leaving soon. I stress to Kris there is no way she will talk me out of it this time. It's not a surprise to them, as I have been planning on leaving since I graduated. Kris does ask me to stay until after the baby is born. I promise Kris that I will stick around for a couple of months to help out while the baby is a newborn.

Kris is bedridden to prevent premature delivery, so I am caring for her as well as the kids. One night, I prepare a full course turkey dinner with all of the trimmings. I am proud of myself. I have come such a long way from those early days when I admitted to Kris that I didn't know how to cook. Fifteen minutes before the food is ready, Kris calls me to her room and says, "Pam, could you please make me tacos for dinner tonight? I just don't feel like turkey."

I am disappointed, because I made the meal with her in mind, hoping she would be proud of my cooking skills.

I am running away from something, although I can't quite name it. I feel dead inside. I don't have a relationship with God. Something isn't right. I have no idea where I fit in. I am lost. I need to get away from everything I have become in L.A. I am nearing thirty, and thoughts of marriage and babies have begun to swirl around my head, yet I have no time with my nanny schedule to even date or have a boyfriend. My minutes, hours, days, and weeks revolve entirely around the people I am working for. I am desperate for a new beginning far away from here.

On November 3, 1995 (two days before Kris turns forty), Kendall Jenner is born. She is the cutest baby girl I've ever seen. Bruce and Kris are ecstatic, and the four kids are overjoyed to have a baby sister. They fight over who gets to hold her. Kendall is the center of attention.

A baby nurse named Jackie starts coming over the day Kendall comes home from the hospital. She is so caring, loving, and kind, and it is nice to have another adult around the house to talk to. Jackie takes wonderful care of Kendall. I'm glad I've already given notice, because I could see myself getting attached to this beautiful baby girl.

CHAPTER TWENTY-SEVEN
Route 66

I go back and forth with plans for the future. I've given my notice and now I have to make a choice about my career and actually leave. One day, I'm certain that being a flight attendant is the right choice, and the next day, I'm ready to commit to moving to Tennessee. Each choice has a list of pros and cons, but they will take me in completely opposite directions. I don't want to make a mistake. This is a huge decision and will be life changing. I'm having such a hard time committing to either one.

January 23, 1996
Dear Dad & Mom,

HI there! Thank you for the long letter and pictures! I loved them. About my life — I know I change my mind every time you hear from me, but I think I've made up my mind that I'm going to move to Tennessee in a few months and manage the convenience store. It will pay better than being a flight attendant. As you can tell, I've been very confused and frustrated as to what to do with my life. I hate making decisions. Well, I'll see you real soon. I'm very excited to be with you.

I love you,
Pam

Although I am leaning heavily towards Tennessee, I am still pursuing a job opportunity with American Airlines (just in case). I have been through numerous rounds of interviews. Kris was a flight attendant for American Airlines for a short time in her early twenties. I ask her for a letter of reference. She writes the most amazing, complimentary letter. When I read it, I can't believe she is talking about me. It brings tears to my eyes. I have no idea she feels this way about me and the job I've done for her all these years. She has *never* said any of these things to me before. It is so nice to finally hear some praise from her, even though it isn't directly from her lips.

February 12, 2006

To Whom It May Concern:

This is a letter of recommendation for Pamela J. Behan. Pamela has worked for our family for the last five years. First, she started out as the Nanny…and as the children have grown older and have longer hours at school, she has made the transition to personal assistant.

The first and foremost thing that stands out about Pamela is her effervescent personality. She is a cheerful, outgoing, sensitive, caring, thoughtful, and truly remarkable human being. She has for the last five years, taken the most precious care of our most treasured possessions…our children. She has demonstrated continuously her remarkable qualities of resourcefulness, dependability, and versatility. She is the most reliable person we have ever had work for us. (And that is saying a lot!) She is always ready for the next assignment, and has the most wonderful attitude…ALWAYS!!! She is extremely adaptable to all situations, and has shown us complete loyalty over the years.

We both spend an incredible amount of time working away from home and are always on an airplane. We certainly know how demanding the job of airline flight attendant is, and we can't think of a more <u>perfect</u> candidate for the position of flight attendant for your airlines than Pamela J. Behan.

The responsibility that she has handled has been enormous. She has demonstrated not only patience, but the ability to cope in any situation and has been the glue that has held our daily lives together. (We're not even sure if she sleeps!) She will be terribly missed.

She has long had the dream of becoming a flight attendant. She wants to travel and see the country. She wants to work with the public, be around people, and work for a credible, successful company such as yours.

We hope you will give consideration to Pamela J. Behan for the position of flight attendant. She is truly **AMAZING** and would be an unbelievable asset to your company.

Best Regards,

Kris and Bruce Jenner

American Airlines finally offers me a position, so I am forced to make a decision. The more I think about the role of flight attendant, it seems as though it may be a lot like being a nanny. You have crazy hours, serve people, and continuously manage problems. I would get to travel, but I'd be working the entire time. And, being on the road constantly with erratic schedules isn't amenable to having a family. I want to get married and start a family. Ultimately, that's my focus and has to be the deciding factor in my decision.

I finally call American Airlines to turn down their job offer. I am heading to Tennessee.

In April 1996, I pile everything I own in my car. I say my final goodbyes to everyone amidst many hugs and tears. Five years have passed since I started as nanny for the Kardashian kids. Kourtney is now seventeen, Kim is fifteen, Khloe is eleven, and Robert is nine. They have grown up under my watchful eye. Kourtney and Kim were little girls when I started, and now they are beautiful young women. Khloe has grown so tall and will be a teenager soon, and I can't call Robert little anymore. He's always been the baby of the family (he was only three when Bruce and Kris met), but he's grown up so much. Five years is a lifetime in a young child's life. They are family to me, and it is heartbreaking to leave them.

Despite the sadness I am feeling, I am also excited to begin my grand, new adventure. So, with tears in my eyes and the wind at my back, I head for my new home — Jackson, Tennessee. I drive across the United States on interstate 40, which used to be Route 66.

Saint Loo-ee; Joplin, Missouri; and Oklahoma City are mighty pretty.
Amarillo; Gallup, New Mexico;
Flagstaff, Arizona; oh, and don't forget Winona.
Kingman, Barstow, San Bernardino.

As I pass through the towns I'd sang about so many times in my musical group, the endless miles of road stretch out before me, providing hours of great "thinking time."

My heart is aching. I am leaving my "family" and feel like I am abandoning them. I have feelings of guilt — as if I am a mother leaving her kids. I am especially worried about Khloe, because we have a special bond. There were many times over the years that she said to me, "You're not going to quit, are you?"

I never lied to her. I would always respond, "Someday, Khloe, but not for a long time."

That someday finally arrived, and I saw in her eyes a sadness that haunts me.

I love those kids, and it is truly difficult to leave them. I was the hired help, and I did the job I was paid to do. But it was so much more than that to me. I poured my heart into my job, and I poured my heart into them. I nurtured them. I cared for them. Hopefully, I made a difference in their lives. I hope they will take a part of me with them. I hope that somehow the years I invested in them will mean something. Whether it's a song that brings a smile of remembrance to their face, some words of encouragement that help them when they are down, or values I've instilled that they find themselves embracing some day. Tears stream down my face as I grieve the loss of "my kids." I *know* it is time to go, but it is not easy to leave.

The sadness is bittersweet, mixing with the nervous excitement and wonder about my new life in Tennessee. I look forward to the adventures that await me, but I'm worried about how I will adjust to the drastic change in culture — from the glamour of Malibu and Beverly Hills to the rural area of Jackson, Tennessee. I'm curious about the new people I will meet and friends I'll make. But, I'm uncertain about the challenge of managing a store and people, which is something I've never done before.

Where will this new road take me?

CHAPTER TWENTY-EIGHT
How's Your Momma-n-Em?

By the end of day two of driving, my back feels as though a million tiny elves are stabbing me with miniature swords. I honestly think I might have to pull over and plant myself in one of the small towns I keep passing through. Find a cheesy motel, drink bad coffee, and eat really greasy diner food for a day or so, until these annoying little people stop torturing me. Despite my daydreams about rest and recovery, I keep pushing through the pain, and finally arrive in Tennessee at my friend's house, where I plan to stay for the first month or so.

I am starting over completely. This trip feels like a rite of passage into another phase of my life. I hope I've made the right choice. I have anxiety about whether this will all work out. I continually remind myself that this is an adventure.

The convenience store is not finished yet, so I am scheduled to train for a couple months at several other convenience stores the owners operate in the area until the new store opens. My very first training location is in Paris, Tennessee. It is not named Paris because it reminded someone of Paris, France. Of this I am certain. *This* Paris is the furthest thing from *that* Paris.

On the morning of my first day, I am greeted by the manager who will be training me. She sticks out her hand to me, smiles and says, "Hi y'all!" Apparently, in the south, they say "y'all" even if they're just talking to one person.

Through her smile, I see that the woman has no front teeth. I shake her hand, hoping the shock I am feeling isn't registering on my face.

170

An hour after I begin my training with her, two policemen walk into the convenience store, not to buy donuts, but to handcuff Ms. Toothless and haul her off to jail for writing bad checks. I look around for a camera. I honestly think I might be on *Candid Camera.* So much for my "professional" training.

The miles between Tennessee and Beverly Hills may as well be light years. This is like a different planet. I miss "my family" back in California, and I am second guessing whether I made the right decision. Is this really where I am supposed to be?

Due to the unexpected departure of the manager, I am promoted immediately to manager of the Paris store, with *zero* training. I learn on the fly.

While I am "training" in Paris, the new site in Jackson is nearing completion. I am often at the construction site, meeting with the construction manager, ordering supplies, and preparing for the opening.

I realize I need help quickly. I talk my friend, Tanya, (whom I've known since childhood) into moving out to Tennessee to be my assistant manager. She does a great job, takes a huge load off of me, and her fun and light-hearted personality keep me sane and laughing in the midst of the craziness.

The construction manager's name is Russell, and his best friend, Ryan, is one of the construction workers at the site.

One day, Russell says, "Pie-am" (Pam has two syllables in the south), "Ryan likes to go to the casinos."

He explains that Ryan often went to Tunica, Mississippi, a town about an hour away that is kind of like a mini Las Vegas, smack in the middle of the green heartland of Mississippi. There are restaurants, buffets, live shows, and casinos. I had begun to notice that Ryan was paying a lot of attention to me, so Russell's comment is an obvious hint that Ryan is indeed interested.

The new store is finally complete, and we open our doors, with me as the manager. The construction of the store cost over a million dollars. We have eight gas pumps in front. Inside the store is a TCBY Yogurt shop and a Broasted Chicken fast food restaurant. We also make fresh submarine sandwiches. At the front of the store is a small dining area with booths, tables and chairs. A section of the store has ready to eat food like hot dogs, corn dogs, nachos, and soft serve ice cream. There are seven or eight aisles, containing grocery, pharmacy, and hardware items. One wall is lined with coolers holding drinks and refrigerated items. Most of these are stocked with beer.

It is crazy, nonstop, heart-pounding insanity from the moment I walk in. A local radio station runs a promotion offering a huge discount on gasoline to the first one hundred customers. Cars are lined up for miles waiting for gas.

I do not sleep a wink for the first forty-eight hours. I am at the store around the clock for two full days. I had no clue going into this endeavor that the store would be so busy, nor that I would be putting out one fire after another. There are problems left and right that require my constant attention.

It is eye opening to me how segregated the area is and the prejudice that still exists. Our store is located on the crosshairs where the black and white areas intersect. I staff my store evenly between blacks and whites to properly serve my customers and keep everyone happy.

Our store is located across the street from many large factories, and all of the factory workers stop by on their way to work, at lunch, on their breaks, and after work. We sell five thousand dollars per day of just beer and cigarettes.

One day, I am in my office, and I notice through the one-way mirror a hand picking up cigarettes and stuffing them in a pocket. I run over to the cigarette aisle and confront the customer.

"Are you going to pay for those cigarettes?" I ask.

"What cigarettes?" he responds, acting innocent.

"The ones you just put in your pocket," I reply, with a firm voice, as I stare him in the face.

He pulls out the cigarettes and heads to the counter to pay.

The store is open twenty-four hours per day and has three different shifts of employees. The headaches involved with managing my employees are like migraines on steroids. The night shift does not have a manager, so there are many calls in the middle of the night. I like my sleep, so this arrangement is getting old quickly. And I don't recall reading "phone calls at all hours of the night" in the fine print of my contract.

One of my busiest shifts is from two to ten p.m. on Fridays. The workers from the factories nearby stop by to cash their checks, and then purchase beer and cigarettes for the weekend.

I was in my apartment one Friday night when I get a call around nine p.m. from my employee Gloria. She is hysterical.

"Pam, oh my gosh. The store was just robbed," she screams through sobs. "It was so horrible. A man came in and he put a gun to my head," she continues, talking so fast I can hardly understand. "He told me to get on the floor. He took the cash."

"Calm down, Gloria. It's okay," I say. "Just try to stay calm, and I will be right there."

I call the police, jump in my car, and race to the store.

When I arrive, she is still very upset. I try to calm her down by having her explain everything again. The police arrive and take a statement from her. I tell Gloria she can head home, and the police leave as well.

I open the safe. It is empty. The store policy is that every employee must do a money drop hourly. This involves taking all of the cash out of the register, with the exception of about a hundred dollars in small bills for change, and depositing it in the slot in the safe.

Gloria was on the afternoon shift from two p.m. until the robbery around nine p.m. on one of our busiest days of the week. There should be thousands of dollars in the safe. I realize Gloria is somehow involved with the robbery.

I go into my office and review the security tapes from the day. There is a camera at the front register. I play the tapes from two p.m. on. I notice at the beginning of the shift, Gloria is talking with a large man who is wearing a black shirt with a huge yellow smiley face on the front. He stands near the counter for a long time, talking to her. When the store gets busy with customers, he goes over to sit down at the dining tables and then heads back over to talk to Gloria again.

I fast forward the tape to about eight thirty p.m., right before the robbery takes place. It is store policy to always have two workers on any given shift. The other worker in the store, who is also a female, suddenly disappears into the freezer and is gone for an inordinately long time. Supposedly stocking shelves, perhaps? Suddenly, I hear a loud "boom, boom, boom," which I can tell is someone banging on the drive through window at the back of the store. A signal? Seconds later, the big guy with the dark t-shirt and yellow smiley face comes into the store. There is no gun and no yelling. He walks up to the counter, and Gloria hands him the money.

My two employees have conspired to rob their own store. I can't believe it.

I call the police, show them the video, and ask them to arrest Gloria. I am shocked when they tell me that they can't arrest her. The tape doesn't prove she's guilty. And, I couldn't fire her. I am so angry and frustrated.

Thankfully, I have a policy in place that if an employee doesn't give adequate notice for their shift, then they are responsible for finding a replacement. If they don't, they are fired. The day after the robbery, Gloria calls me two hours before her shift and says, "I'm too shaken up, I can't come in."

She does not find a replacement, and I fire her the same day.

It is a rude awakening about the reality of my position. What did I get myself into? Frequently, I am running frantically around the store, dealing with ten issues at once and observing the country bumpkin folk traipsing through my store, and the thought pops into my head, I wonder what Kris and Bruce and the kids are doing right now? I recall my life in Hollywood — driving the Land Cruiser, shopping in Beverly Hills, and picking up lunch at Spago's. That world already seems so far away.

I romanticized my move to Tennessee, imagining beautiful countryside, a nice southern gentleman, and a horse farm. I based my impressions on the state solely on my trip to Nashville with Linda and the boys. Nashville is urban, the people are more sophisticated, there is more to do, and of course our accommodations were first class. Living in a fairly small town in a rural area of Tennessee is a far cry from Nashville. I experience culture shock on a daily basis. I try to have a good sense of humor about it. I take pictures of street signs to send to my mom, such as Peckerwood Point and Lizard Lick. There's a town nearby called Bucksnort. I don't think I could live in a place called Bucksnort.

Ryan comes by the store several times to ask me out on a date. He is so much younger than me (I'm twenty-eight and he's twenty-one), and I have no interest wasting my time with someone who isn't ready for marriage, so I tell him no.

The boy is persistent. He continues to stop by the store every few days to ask me out. One day, I've had enough of it.

I turn to face him directly and say, "Look, Ryan. I'm twenty-eight. You're twenty-one. I'm ready to get married, settle down, and have kids. Are you?"

He doesn't respond. He looks at me for a moment, then turns around and walks away. Well, that takes care of that.

Early the next morning, I am in my office with the door wide open. In walks Ryan, with a very serious expression on his face. He closes the door behind him, faces me, and hands me an index card. I look at it and realize he has written out all the words to a Fleetwood Mac song titled "Don't Stop." The main lyric of the chorus is "don't stop thinking about tomorrow."

He says, simply, "Yep. I'm ready."

I am flabbergasted. I asked the question. He took his time to think about it and then gave me a serious answer. Since he took me seriously, I think maybe I should take him seriously, so I agree to go on one date with him.

One date becomes two dates, and before I realize what is happening, we are an item. I like him, and it is a great distraction from the store.

Not long after I meet Ryan, I decide to start attending church again. As I walk through the doors of a church not far from my apartment, I feel a rush of emotion. I haven't been inside a church in so many years. I choose a seat in the very back, because I don't want anyone to see me cry. It feels like home. Like eating Mom's warm homemade apple pie at the kitchen table with my family. It is familiar and comfortable. I start attending every Sunday, and tears stream down my cheeks, as I process feelings of guilt and regret.

I don't connect with the people in the church. I'm not quite ready for that. I come and go silently, always sitting in the back of the church. My life seems so messed up. I'm not at a place where I can share all my "junk" with other people. I do feel the presence of God, which is something new to me. For the first time, I start to feel some kind of a connection with Him. I don't really know what I am feeling, and I can't put it into words. I just know that it is different than the judgmental God on a throne in the sky I'd known as a child.

In the fall of 1997, Ryan and I are at my apartment one night, sitting on the couch. We have been dating for over a year.

"So, you really wanna get married?" he asks.

"Yes, I really do," I reply.

He pulls out a ring that he had hidden under the cushions of the couch and puts it on my finger.

"Will you marry me, Pie-am?" The country boy asks me, in his Southern drawl.

I pause, and in that moment a torrent of thoughts rush through my head. Yes, I really do want to get married, although I'm not quite sure you are the one I want to get married to. But, I can't imagine saying no when he's obviously so nervous and has put thought and effort into this proposal. Just say yes for now and we can figure the rest out as we go.

"Yes!" I exclaim, with a bright smile that hides my uncertainty.

Part of me is so happy that my dream of becoming a wife and mother will be coming true. That is really all I ever wanted for myself — a happy little family. Getting married seems like a pretty good solution to fixing my life and doing the right thing. I am about to turn thirty. It is time to start a family, and here is someone who wants me.

We begin planning our wedding, but whenever Ryan presses me to set a date, I can't commit. I keep putting it off. I am unsure of many things about Ryan.

I have begun to notice that our socializing revolves around partying and drinking. His mom has twelve brothers and sisters that live in the area, and the family gets together often, which usually involves heavy drinking. I begin to blame Ryan's drinking on his family and friends — his environment — instead of holding him accountable. One night, I am disgusted with how drunk he is and his behavior. The next morning, I confront him.

"Ryan, I'm breaking up with you. I'm moving back to Rapid City."

The idea has been forming in my head for a while. My mom and dad purchased a second home (a farm) near Aberdeen, South Dakota, in recent years, and my brother lives in South Dakota, as well. I went to college in Rapid City and really liked the city, so it seems like a good choice for my next move. I can be in a city that I already know and where I have some friends, yet also be close to my family.

I am fed up with the continuous headaches of managing the convenience store. I have been working there for almost two years now, and still receive calls from my staff at all hours of the day and night. I am tired of working at the store. I am tired of Ryan's drinking. I am fed up with everything about Tennessee. It is time to leave.

Ryan is very upset when I tell him about my decision. He begs and pleads and swears to me that he will quit drinking. He says he wants to move back to South Dakota with me and start a new life.

I believe him.

On July 4, 1998, we pack up all of our belongings in a rented trailer and head back to South Dakota.

Two days later, we drive into Rapid City, get out of the car, and stand up. We both pass out on the ground because of the extreme altitude change.

Ryan and I rent a cute little house on a quaint street in suburban Rapid City. The neighborhood is full of families and children. It seems like a perfect place to start our new life together.

He gets a job working at the local ACE hardware store. I interview with an investment company called Waddell and Reed, figuring I'd follow my father's and brother's footsteps into the insurance business. Before I can become an insurance and investment rep, I have to pass two extremely difficult tests called the Series 6 and Series 66. I have never been very business minded, didn't pay too much attention in math, and wasn't so good at studying either, so this is quite a challenge for me.

I take the first test in early fall 1998 — driving five hours to Sioux Falls to sit for the test — and fail miserably. I have to wait thirty days before I can retake it. We are living off the meager salary Ryan makes at the hardware store, while I wait to retake the test. I fail again the second time by only one point. Another thirty day wait, and another thirty days of studying. Third time's the charm. I finally pass. I am scheduled to begin working as an insurance rep at Waddell and Reed in January 1999. All the fragments completing my vision of a perfect life seem to be falling into place. Now for one major piece of the puzzle…

CHAPTER TWENTY-NINE
Going to the Chapel

On November 28, 1998, Ryan and I are married in my hometown of Norcross, Minnesota, in the small white church with a steeple where I'd attended church throughout my childhood. My wedding is the very last wedding held in the church before they close it. The congregation is simply too small. Too many people have moved away. But on my wedding day, the little church is filled to overflowing with my family and friends. Not many of Ryan's friends or family could afford to fly out to Minnesota. But, we have planned to go back to Tennessee for a reception.

The ceremony is beautiful, my dress is gorgeous, the flowers are perfect, and I am surrounded by all the people I love most in the world. What more could a girl want? Despite my happiness, which is truly genuine, there are glimmers of doubt below the surface. Here I am about to embark on the most important new chapter in my life, yet in the deepest part of my heart I have to admit that I have some serious reservations about Ryan.

Our reception is held at a hotel in the town of Morris, Minnesota, which is about thirty minutes from the church. I have many dear childhood and high school friends at the wedding, many whom I hadn't seen in years, and I am the epitome of a social butterfly. I am in my element, talking to everyone, catching up, having fun, dancing, and laughing.

Ryan doesn't have any friends or family at the wedding. He is friendly enough, but other than my family, he knows no one at the wedding. He is pretty much on his own. With me busy socializing, I guess he sees it as a ticket to drink as much as possible. Which is exactly what he does.

He is so drunk. Stumbling drunk. He passes out the minute we get back to our room after the reception and dance. I lie on the bed in our hotel room, wide-awake and alone, staring at the ceiling. With a sickening feeling in my stomach, I look over at the man passed out next to me, realizing I have made a huge mistake.

This is how my marriage begins.

And so it continues.

Despite his promises before we moved from Tennessee, Ryan still finds many reasons and opportunities to drink. Yet, I love him. Enough for both of us, I hope. I truly believe that if I stand by him, he will eventually turn around. I hope he loves me enough to change.

Promises made, and long ago forgotten, my life moves forward day by day, as I struggle with Ryan's alcoholism. I bury myself in my new job, forging relationships with clients and co-workers, willing myself to be happy and make the best of it.

I do whatever I can to supplement our meager income. We are both paid commission only, so it is a constant struggle. Before long, we have racked up charges on our credit card. I give piano lessons and take on, not one, but *three* different paper routes every morning, which requires I get up at the ungodly hour of four o'clock.

I begin attending a Lutheran church, and eventually accept a job as church organist to help me pay the bills. I have become accustomed to the regular time with God. The messages I hear seep into my heart, and bring some element of comfort, although I don't feel that much different about God than before. It is something that I do on Sundays. It feels good. I love the inspirational messages. I'm going to church. I'm praying, but it doesn't change much with Ryan.

I am struggling to make our relationship work. I drag Ryan along to church, trying to lead him to God, and hoping that will solve our problems. I try so hard to make him a Christian.

As a way of coping, or maybe to forget, or perhaps to pretend that it is all going to be okay, I decide to go ahead and try to have a baby. I'd always wanted to be a mother and think maybe a baby will make things better. Or at the very least, I'll have another little being to love and it will help me to overlook Ryan's issues.

After a year at Waddell and Reed, I move over to work for New York Life, one of the most prestigious insurance companies. After my first year, I am named New Agent of the Year. I drop the paper routes, as I am beginning to do quite well in the insurance industry. At least my career is going well.

Somewhere into the second year of trying to get pregnant, we begin to realize there might be a problem. I schedule appointments for both Ryan and myself to get tested, to see if either of us might be the problem. The results come back negative. There is no medical reason why we aren't getting pregnant.

Desperate at this point to have a baby, we turn to fertility treatments. I begin taking fertility pills, to try to assist my body in getting pregnant. They don't work. We keep trying. We never resort to IVF, mainly because of the cost. I pray every night that God will give me the gift of a baby, but week after week, month after month, year after year, those prayers remained unanswered.

It is devastating to me. Every month, I am filled with hope that *this* will be the month I am pregnant, and then I get my period, and those hopes are dashed into a million jagged pieces. I want a child with every fiber of my being, and it is so frustrating that there is no explanation for why I can't get pregnant.

I spent so many years taking care of other people's children. I always thought some day I would have my own. It is so painful, and I don't understand why this is happening to me. I ask God over and over....why?

CHAPTER THIRTY
Sweet Reunion

In July 2000, my parents and I fly to Los Angeles to attend Smitty's wedding. I am one of the bridesmaids. I have stayed in touch with Bruce, Kris, and the kids, and make plans to meet up with them.

My parents and I drive to Beverly Hills to spend some time with Bruce and Kris. It is so good to see both of them after being gone four years. Kendall is four, and Kylie (whom I've never met) is about to turn three. They are the cutest little girls, with dark hair and eyes like their mom, and porcelain skin.

Kris says, "Wait until you see Khloe. She looks like a Victoria's Secret model."

A few minutes later, Khloe walks down the stairs, and I am astonished by her appearance. She is now sixteen, tall and slender. Her hair is light brown, and she wears it long and straightened. She looks gorgeous.

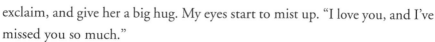

"Khloe, you look so beautiful! I can't believe how tall you are," I exclaim, and give her a big hug. My eyes start to mist up. "I love you, and I've missed you so much."

It is an emotional reunion. I can't believe how grown up my little girl is now.

Before long, the front door opens, and Kim walks in. I am stunned by her beauty. Her hair is incredibly long, dark, shiny, and perfectly straight. She wears a low cut tank top, dark pants, and a gold cuff around her upper arm. She looks glamorous and sexy. It's impossible not to notice how curvy she has become. I am amazed at how she has matured in four years.

Early the next morning, I meet Khloe and Robert at a restaurant for breakfast. Khloe recently started driving, and my little Robert is no longer little. When I left he was still a little boy with chubby cheeks. He is now thirteen, and has grown so tall and thin. I give him a big hug, and tell him how happy I am to see him. We laugh, talk, and joke, remembering all the fun we used to have.

I'm not sure if I am going to have time to get together with Kourtney due to all of the wedding activities. I ask if she can come to the hair salon in Thousand Oaks where I am getting my hair done later that morning, and she agrees.

Kourtney picks up Khloe and meets me at the salon. Kourtney is twenty-one, and she has blossomed into such a beautiful young lady. Her hair is long as well, and straight. She seems so confident and grown up.

One of the first things Kourtney says is, "I hear that song you like on the radio all the time."

I know immediately she is referring to Gloria Estefan's, "I Live for Loving You." I told her years ago she would someday hear the song and think of Nanny Pam.

"And you miss me, don't you?" I ask.

A huge grin covers her face, but she doesn't say anything.

They stay with me at the salon while I get my hair done, which takes about an hour. We catch up on each other's lives, laugh, and joke. It feels just like old times.

It is a fun trip, and I'm so thankful I get to reunite with "my kids." I am so proud of the young people they have become.

CHAPTER THIRTY-ONE
When it Rains, it Pours

The days, weeks, months, and years fly by as I deal with my sad and lonely marriage. I continue to try to get pregnant, hoping I will be blessed with a baby that can either save my marriage or at least give me something else to focus on. I bury myself in work, and my insurance business continues to flourish. It is small consolation though, because my personal life is in turmoil.

To make matters worse, I am devastated to find out that my father is not doing well. From the time I was a little girl, my vision of my father included a pipe in his mouth. He loved to smoke that pipe. Unfortunately, after a lifetime of smoking, my father developed severe emphysema.

In July of 2003, my parents drive to California so my dad can undergo special laser treatments to remove the affected lung tissue. Something goes wrong after the surgery, as my dad's lungs will not heal. One of his lungs collapses, there are constant setbacks, and he barely survives.

I fly out to Los Angeles and stay with them in their hotel for a few days. Ryan stays home. It is stressful seeing my dad so ill, but we are hopeful that he will get better. At least this surgery will buy him some time. I think my parents have figured out that my relationship with Ryan is on the rocks. But for the most part, I haven't burdened them with the details, because they are going through so much.

After four and a half months in and out of the hospital, my parents are finally able to return home to Minnesota. Despite a long healing process, the surgery seems to be a success, as my dad enjoys a much-improved quality of life. They caution, however, that it is a temporary solution that will last about three years.

Ryan's drinking continues and escalates. After six and a half years of marriage, I finally realize he is not going to change. I resent him for drinking. When he does have a stint of sobriety, he resents me that he isn't drinking. The resentment in our marriage is so thick, we can't see through it to find the love or friendship that brought us together in the first place. I begin to think about divorce but find it hard to take that final step.

One night in the fall of 2004, Ryan takes the fateful final step for me. He hits me. If they hit you once, they *will* hit you again. I know that. In a way, I am relieved that it happened, because now I can *finally* justify leaving him.

A month later, Ryan flies back home by himself to Tennessee for Christmas. While he is home, surrounded by his family and friends, I call him and tell him I am going to file for divorce. He doesn't argue or protest. He already knew.

Divorce is never easy, but this one is relatively cordial. I think Ryan missed his family, his friends, and his life back in Tennessee, and he seems excited to be back home in the country.

He flies back to Rapid City after Christmas, and I move out of our house for a week so he can go through our belongings and pack. We are fair about splitting our possessions. He leaves me with all of the furniture. The only thing he really insists on taking is our beloved springer spaniel, Smokey.

At the end of the week, Ryan calls.

"I'm sitting in the Kmart parking lot," he says softly. "Do you want to come by and say goodbye?"

"Yes, I do," I reply, as tears come to my eyes.

I quickly drove over to Kmart. We both get out of our cars, and without a word, embrace in a long hug.

"Bye," I whisper through tears.

"Bye," he replies, turns, gets in his car, and drives off.

What else can be said? It is over.

I get into my car and sit there for a while, lost in thought. An overwhelming sadness envelops me, as I feel the loss way down deep in my marrow, the regret of what might have been, the years forever lost.

As I drive away, the Fleetwood Mac song, "Don't Stop" comes on the radio (the song he had written on the index cards). I call him on my cell to tell him. It is a bittersweet moment — a stark contrast between what was good back then and the finality of this unhappily ever after.

It is strange timing, because that song, in a way, is what started our relationship. He wrote out the lyrics, because he wanted me to think about "tomorrow" — a future with him. Now here it is playing on the radio at the end of our relationship, and it represents something completely different — a future without him.

I did a whole lot of praying over the past six and a half years. I had asked God a million and one times to improve our relationship, help Ryan with his drinking issues, and to give us a baby. I had gotten to know God much better simply because of the huge amount of time I'd spent talking to him. He had become more personal to me. Yet, despite my newfound connection with God, I feel a void in my heart, and a deep desire to have someone love me the way I hope to be loved.

Not long after Ryan moves back to Tennessee, my neighbor Terry, with whom both Ryan and I had become friendly, starts flirting with me in a fairly obvious way. He shovels snow off my driveway and sidewalks, helps me out with odd jobs I need done around the yard and the house, and comes over to chat whenever he sees that I am home.

I am starving for affection and love. Terry says all the right things, and makes me *feel* loved. I eat up the attention. He is a fun person, and we get along great. It is much too convenient with him living only two doors down from my house.

Without much thought or discernment, I start a romance with Terry not long after Ryan leaves. Even if there was a huge stamp on his forehead reading "rebound relationship" I don't think I could have stopped myself. I know in my heart it is too soon, but I can't acknowledge it. It feels too good. After years of feeling nothing, feeling *something* matters more than the heartbreak I know deep in my soul is sure to follow.

In April 2005, I notice a spot on my left upper arm that looks like ringworm. After watching it for a few weeks, I realize it isn't going away, so I make an appointment to see my dermatologist. Terry, who has become my constant companion, goes with me. When my female doctor enters the room, Terry flirts with her so obviously that I am actually a bit embarrassed for him. I dismiss the disrespect to me, thinking, he's just a flirt.

My doctor takes one look at the spot, and says, "Pam, this is cancer. You're coming back tomorrow morning."

Terry goes with me again the next morning. As we sit in the doctor's waiting room, I am looking through a magazine and see a picture of a gorgeous wedding ring.

Terry notices. "You like that?"

"I love it," I reply.

"You want me to get you one?"

"Sure!"

I mean it. I am in love again, and caught up in the newness of the relationship. My knight in shining armor is saving me, the damsel in distress, as I deal with cancer. I buy the whole romantic scenario — hook, line, and sinker.

Learning about my diagnosis was scary. I am worried the cancer may have spread or it may reoccur. It makes me think about how precious life is and how short. I feel vulnerable. I don't want to go through this alone. I open my heart wide and invest myself completely into my relationship with Terry.

Later that day, after spending most of the day at the doctor's office, we are at Terry's house, and he surprises me with a pepper steak sandwich he made himself. When we finish eating, he tosses me a ring, and asks, "Want to marry me?"

I dismiss the lackluster of his half-hearted proposal, telling myself, that's just Terry's personality. I say yes, proudly put the ring on my finger, and move forward with the intention that we will someday be married.

Our engagement presents one big issue, however. My family. They simply won't understand. Both Terry and I know this is true love. The real deal. But, I doubt my parents will believe that, since I just separated from my husband.

"We have to wait," I announce.

"But you want kids and I want kids. I don't want to wait," he retorts.

"We have to wait," I firmly state again.

"You're not getting any younger," he rationalizes.

I am thirty-six, and my biological clock is not only ticking very loudly, but setting off blaring alarms. I assume I can't get pregnant, after trying unsuccessfully for six years. We reach an agreement of sorts. We will wait to get married, but we agree to have unprotected sex, and hope for a baby. It will buy me some time to tell my parents about my new relationship.

Being diagnosed with cancer makes me more willing to take risk and throw caution to the wind. I am in love, and that is all that matters.

One day, I am flicking through the channels on television, and to my great surprise, I see Brandon and Brody. They (along with Linda and David Foster) are on a reality television show called *The Princes of Malibu*. I can't believe it. I watch in amazement. It is the first time I have seen them in many years, and I am surprised how grown up they are. Brandon and Brody are handsome boys. Linda looks exactly the same, and as beautiful as ever. It's hard to believe that my boys are now television stars.

It seems like a lifetime ago that I was their nanny. My life is so different now.

Between April and October, I begin to notice a lot of ups and downs in Terry's behavior. Sometimes, he has so much energy that he exhausts me. Occasionally, he won't even go to bed. He stays up all night, fiddling around in the garage. He takes things apart that don't need to be taken apart. He cleans things that don't need to be cleaned. I try to keep up with him, but it is impossible.

Then, inevitably, he crashes, and sleeps for three days straight. After noticing this drastic behavior for several months, I ask him about it.

"Oh yeah. I never really wanted to tell you about it, but I'm bipolar," Terry admits.

The next day, I call an insurance client of mine who I know is bipolar and describe Terry's symptoms. He confirms that it sounds exactly like bipolar symptoms.

That night, I try to talk to him about it.

"Terry, why don't you get on meds?"

"I'm not going to get addicted to any meds," he retorts, irritated at my response, and walks away.

For months, I pay two mortgage payments — mine and his. He always has an excuse for why he can't pay. Finally, I decide to sell my house, and move in with him, so we only have one mortgage. We are practically living together anyway, so it seems like a good move.

In early November, Terry and I have a horrible fight. I catch him talking to another girl on the phone, and demand that I meet her, if she is "just a friend" as he says. He refuses. I move out and stay with a friend, Judy, for two weeks, trying to figure out what I am going to do.

On November 18, I am in my car driving over to Terry's house to tell him I am breaking up with him. I am listening to the local Christian radio station.

The announcer says, "Are you about to give up on someone? Don't give up on someone too soon. Jesus forgave seven times seventy."

Is this message meant for me?

My period is late, but I have been late countless times all those years I tried to get pregnant, only to be disappointed time and time again. So I haven't taken a pregnancy test yet.

After hearing the message, which seems like a sign from God, I decide to pull over and buy a pregnancy test to see if I am indeed pregnant. I want to know *before* I go to see Terry. I buy a test at a drug store and go into the bathroom of a nearby convenience store.

It is positive. I am both happy and sad. Happy because this has been my deepest desire for years. Yet, sad because my relationship has been so rocky lately, and here I am finding out this wonderful news by myself in the bathroom of a convenience store.

I sit in my car for a long time, thinking everything over. I have a new life growing in my tummy. I want this child to have what I had — a mommy and daddy who love each other and who live in the same home. I have to give Terry another shot, for the sake of my baby. My drive over to see Terry and break up has been sidelined by a message on the radio and now switches to a completely different focus.

When I arrive at Terry's house, I sit him down and ask him, "Are you willing to do *anything* to make this relationship work?"

"Yes, I am, Pam," he promises, seeming remorseful.

I'd heard about a Christian couples retreat called "A Weekend to Remember," which happens to be coming up that weekend. I ask Terry if he will go with me. He agrees, so I tell him that I will pick him up at his house on Friday. I say nothing about being pregnant.

When I arrive at his house on Friday, I hand him a card with baby blocks on the front. On the inside, I have written, "Congratulations. Hope you and mommy work things out because I really want to be a part of both of your lives."

He looks at me with a startled expression and asks, "What does this mean?"

"I'm pregnant," I reply.

Terry bursts into tears. I am so touched by his tears and how happy he seems. I believe in my heart that somehow everything will work out.

I agree to get back together and work on our relationship, although I decide to continue living with my girlfriend until I am sure Terry is committed to making things work.

On December 1, 2005, I receive a call on my cell phone from a parole officer who informs me that Terry has been arrested for possession of Methamphetamines. A girl named Theresa was with him at the time of the arrest. I feel like I have been kicked in my stomach. I am a few weeks pregnant, and the father of my baby is with another woman. I know what it means. Everything makes sense now. The phone calls. The "friend" I can't meet. The erratic behavior and mood swings.

I drive to the jail the next day to talk to him. The Meth possession and drug use should be a huge concern for me and I definitely need explanation and some show of remorse. First and foremost, I care about one thing, and I have only one question.

"Were you sleeping with her?"

Acting offended that I'd even suggest such a thing, he responds, "No, Pam, I swear on the Bible. I swear on my unborn child's life. I was not sleeping with her. I have never slept with her. She was just my drug connection."

Again, I believe him. I want so badly for this to work. I want to trust the love I feel for him. I want to believe he loves me, and that he can change, and that I can help him change. I trust him, and I begin to plan how I will manage this pregnancy alone until he's out of prison, and we can all be a family again.

I have been attending the same church (Atonement Lutheran Church) since I moved to Rapid City in 1998, and I am still the organist. I've been a regular, faithful member, but it sure hasn't kept my life from falling apart. In a way, I guess it's not much different from the church experience of my youth. I go because I know I should. It does make me feel better when I attend. The people are nice, the pastor is great, and the messages are inspiring. But I don't read the Bible, I'm not involved in any study groups, and I don't pray all that much except when I really need God's help for something.

I am worried about telling the pastor and the church members about my pregnancy. I'm not sure how they will treat me. I doubt they will want me to be the organist anymore.

Their reaction overwhelms me. Every single member of the church showers me with love, acceptance, support, and kindness. I need a place to stay because Terry's house is being sold. One of the members lets me live in the apartment in their basement, for drastically reduced rent, which is such a blessing.

I believe in my heart that God put Terry in my life for a reason. I have suffered deep hurt, but I am willing to stand by him if this is God's purpose for me, and if I am supposed to be the one to lead him to God. I wonder to myself if I am too loyal. It's always been something I pride myself on. I was loyal to my first boyfriend in high school, I was loyal to the Jenners and Kardashians. I was loyal to Ryan for seven years, and now I'm staying loyal to Terry. I have to believe that he wants to get better and that he is committed to our relationship.

Now I have to tell my parents, and I dread calling them. They don't even know I'm dating someone, and now I have to confess I'm pregnant too. I finally gather the courage and call them. My dad's response is, "Well, the damage is done." Not exactly supportive. Of course they have questions about the father of the baby. I can't bring myself to tell them the truth, so I concoct a huge lie. I tell them Terry has received a civilian contract over in Iraq to work on a construction project and that he is overseas for my entire pregnancy.

The main reason I lie is because of my dad's illness. For years, he has become progressively sicker, short of breath, and unable to do the things that he loved. I know the truth about Terry will upset him so much, and I fear it will affect his health, so I lie to try to protect my father.

I support Terry as he is sentenced and sent away to prison. And, I support him by driving to visit him once a month, my tummy getting bigger and bigger. I don't have much money, and every trip with food, gas, and hotel is at least a hundred dollars. My first pregnancy — an event I have looked forward to my whole life — should be a joyous time of celebration, expectation, and sharing every little new development with my partner. Instead, I am alone.

I am broken. My life is in shambles. I am disappointed in myself and my choices. The dreams I had for my life have been shattered, the broken shards trampled in the mud. I have a big belly. I am an unwed mother. My boyfriend — the father of my baby — is in jail. I am lying to my family. I can't get much lower unless I start crawling. I am feeling pretty sorry for myself, lonely, and quite unlovable.

And then the kind people at my church show me just how lovable I am. One of the ladies at the church, Eldene, hosts a baby shower for me at her house. I think every lady in that church attends, even women I had never met. I will have everything I need when my baby is born, thanks to them. Women from the church often call to check up on me, ask if I need to talk, and invite me to lunch. I am overwhelmed at how these kind people are treating me — an unwed mother whose partner is in jail (which churches generally frowned upon, or so I thought). It is exactly what I would hope for from people who follow the teachings of Jesus. It is above and beyond what I ever imagined or expected.

Their actions change my life and transform my faith in God. It is a defining moment in my life and in my walk with God. They show me what the true love of Jesus looks like. And through them, I experience His love, in a real and tangible way. It isn't just empty words in a book. It is real. It makes me want more of Him and expect more from Him. I want to personally know a God who can love me like that.

So I join a Bible study. I am lying on my bed, after coming home from my first night of Bible study. I open up the front of my Bible, after blowing the dust off the cover. As I gingerly turn the thin pages, I notice one verse highlighted on the title page. Wow, this must be a really important verse, I think. The verse is Isaiah 40:8, *"The grass withers, the flower fades, but the word of the Lord stands forever."* Flowery and lovely, but I don't quite get what it means.

So I open the study book we will be going through. And at the top of the page for the first lesson is a Bible verse: 1st Peter 1: 24-25. *"All people are like grass, and all their glory is like the flower of the field; the grass withers and the flowers fall, but the word of the Lord endures forever."*

Whoa! That gets my attention. I feel like God is speaking directly to me. Okay, so I guess the word of God — the Bible — is rather important. I make a commitment right there to start reading the Bible regularly.

That's how it starts — my real relationship with God. First, I came to know that God loved me through the actions of the people in my church. Secondly, I hear God speak to me directly through two Bible verses about grass and flowers. And, finally, I begin to read God's words to me from the

Bible. That is how my true, real, deep down in my soul, "relationship" with God begins. Pretty simple really, yet so profound.

Lying to my parents is taking its toll on me. It is a constant source of guilt, stress, and regret. But my father's condition continues to deteriorate, and as much as I want to unburden my heart and tell them the truth, I don't want to be the cause of stress for him. He would be angry and heartbroken, and he would worry constantly about me.

The laser treatment my father underwent in California in 2003 was a temporary solution, and now the emphysema is back with a vengeance. In the early part of 2006, we begin discussing the possibility of a lung transplant. There are so many potential complications, but it is beginning to look like that might be the only option for my dad, as he has become so sick.

My beautiful, precious son is born on August 2, 2006. My mom is with me for the delivery, and it is a wonderful blessing to share the experience with her. I am sad that my dad (who is too sick to travel) can't be here to welcome his new grandson into the world. A few minutes after my son is born, as they lay him in my arms, I look up at my mom, and I can hardly get the words out between my tears.

"Mom, his name is going to be James."

My mom bursts into tears. I have kept the name a secret all of these months. He is named James Terry Behan after my father. His nickname will be Jamie, a name I've liked since I was a little girl. A few minutes later, my mom calls my dad, but she has a hard time telling him because my dad is so emotional. He is elated.

I am thrilled that Jamie is born on August 2nd, because it is the same date I caught the huge walleye I told Brandon and Brody about. It was the most significant moment of my youth, and now the most important event of my adult life has happened on the same day.

During my pregnancy, I walked a couple miles every morning. While I walked, I would pray, "Dear God, I'm okay with my baby being a boy or girl, whatever you think would bless me and my family the most. I pray that he or she would look like whichever parent it would benefit the most, and I pray that it will be healthy."

God knew what he was doing. It is so special that I was able to name him after my father. As for looks, he is the spitting image of me.

When Jamie is only a month old, I take my tiny newborn son to meet his dad in jail. I continue to make these trips every month, even in the frigid cold South Dakota winter. I believe it is the right thing to do. I blindly trust that Terry wants to overcome his drug use, and I am holding on to the belief that he did not cheat on me.

When Terry gets out of prison on January 11, 2007, I am thrilled to be back together. He moves into the condo I purchased the previous spring. I truly believe he is on a straight path to recovery. He regularly attends a Narcotics Anonymous class. I begin to harbor hope in my heart that my dreams of a happy family life are finally going to come true.

In March of 2007, my dad is so deathly ill that a lung transplant becomes his only option for survival. He is admitted to the Gift of Life Transplant House in Rochester, Minnesota, right next to the Mayo Clinic, to wait for a lung to become available. On May 7th, we get the call that a lung is available, and the next day my dad receives his new lung.

After a stay in the hospital, and three more months back at the Gift of Life Transplant House for recovery, my dad goes home — with a new lease on life. I've never seen my father so happy and carefree. He is like a little kid with a happy go lucky attitude. He can be active again and do the things he loves.

He can breathe freely again. It is so nice to see my dad back to his old self. I hope and pray there will be no complications. My parents have been through so much in the last few years because of his illness.

My parents and I visit each other often, and they bond with their grandson. My mom and dad adore little Jamie, and love spending time with him. It melts my heart to see how my dad lights up when Jamie is around him.

While that part of my life is looking up, Terry's carefully crafted lies and deceit finally catch up to him. I find out for certain that he has been cheating on me since the beginning of our relationship. I yell, scream, rant, and rave. I didn't know I was capable of feeling so much anger and hate towards another human being. Everything I went through the last year and a half was one big lie. I visited him in jail for a year, brought my newborn son to see him in the dead of winter, sent him money so he could call me every day, lied to my parents while my dad was near death, and, worst of all, believed in him. I *always* believed in him.

I kick Terry out of my home the day I find out.

It all makes sense now. A thousand images flood my mind, as I piece together the web of betrayal and deceit. I think about the day he proposed. I can't believe how callous and indifferent he acted, and how naïve and gullible I was. I desired to be loved so badly, that I put blinders on, and saw only what I wanted to see. I was pretty naïve about the whole thing. The truth is that I'd never been around drugs or anyone who was addicted to drugs. Looking back now, I think, You idiot! How could you not know? Towards the end, before his tightly wound ball of lies and deception began to unwind, I think I did know, but I didn't want it to be true. I loved him so much.

That night, as I am lying in bed thinking, I recall for the first time some words of wisdom I heard many years before, from my old friend, Sylvester Stallone. "DTA. Don't trust anyone. Just give it twenty years, and you won't trust anyone either," Sly said to me that day as we stood in his closet. It has been almost twenty years, and my heart has been broken one too many times. I promise myself that night, "Don't Trust Anyone" will be my new motto when it comes to men.

CHAPTER THIRTY-TWO
Goodbye, Daddy

The joy of my dad's new lease on life with his transplanted lung is short lived. Because strong drugs must be administered to prevent the body from rejecting the new lung, the immune system is compromised. As a result, a complication (although rare) with lung transplants is another form of cancer, called post transplant lymphoma. A couple of months after he returns home, my father receives the devastating news that he has this form of cancer. Based on the doctor's advice, my parents decided to pursue chemotherapy treatments, with the knowledge that there is only a forty percent chance that it will actually work.

We are able to enjoy the summer together, my father loving his new role as Grandpa to Jamie. I take many pictures of them together. Jamie loves his grandpa so much.

Terry has become a fugitive. He violates his parole and hasn't been seen in months. As I'm driving to the store one day with my young son in his car seat in the back, I see a huge billboard at the side of the road reading, "WANTED." And there in black and white, larger than life, is the sullen face of my son's father. I look at Jamie, who is chewing on a toy.

"There's your daddy," I say, and turn around quickly so he can't see the tears running down my cheeks.

How did this happen? How did my dreams for my life, marriage and motherhood end up so twisted and distorted? This is not what I wanted for myself or for my child. I am devastated for my son, who coos contentedly in the backseat. He is oblivious to his situation now. He knows only that he has a mommy that loves him and protects him. But someday he will know. Someday I will have to tell him. I can see the future of this man on the billboard, and I no longer expect change nor hope for more. And I cry hot, bitter tears for the inevitable moments of truth, sadness and longing that will someday encircle my precious son.

On October 28, 2007, my 39th birthday, my dad and brother take a hunting trip together, knowing it will likely be the last one for my father. My dad calls to share his good news that he shot a deer with his bow and arrow. It is a special moment to for him and me. I will never forget how excited he was to tell me. Hunting and fishing have been the great loves of my father's life, and it is nice he is able to end the last hunting season with a victory.

A few days later, my dad is readmitted to the Mayo Clinic, as the cancer takes its toll, to begin chemotherapy. In January of 2008, he is well enough to make a trip home to Norcross, but the visit is cut short when he is rushed to a hospital in nearby Alexandria, because he has contracted pneumonia.

My friend, Carol, who is a very spiritual woman and seems to have a close connection to God, has been encouraging me to talk to my dad about his relationship with Jesus before he dies. My own spiritual life has become my priority, and I want to make sure that my dad knows Jesus personally.

My parents have always gone to church, but I've never discussed my dad's religious beliefs with him before. Now I am concerned, since he is nearing the end of his life. I want and need to know he is in a good place spiritually.

"If you don't talk to him, you will never forgive yourself, Pam. You'll always wonder," Carol cautions.

At the hospital, my mom watches Jamie so I can spend some time alone with my dad.

I sit down next to his bed, noticing how frail and fragile he looks. I grasp his hand and say, "Daddy we're about to leave. I hope you have a good night."

He responds, "It's going to take a lot more than a good night."

"You're right, Dad," I reply. "There's nothing I want more in the whole world than for you to see Jamie grow up. It devastates me that you may not be around to see that. But Daddy you've fought such a hard battle. If you're tired, and you want

to go home, Jesus is waiting for you." I pause, wiping away the tears rolling down my cheeks, and then continue.

"Do you know he's waiting for you?"

He starts to cry.

"Yes," he whispers.

I continue, "Dad, I don't know if you've done it. But all you have to do is ask him into your heart and you're there."

"I have."

I smile and hug him tight. When I leave the room, I feel complete peace, knowing my father is going to be okay, no matter what happens next.

He is transferred straight from the hospital in Alexandria back to the Mayo Clinic. We know his time is short, as the cancer continues to spread. Chemo isn't helping.

I am visiting him in early April. One day, as I am sitting with him, I read a verse out of a devotional book of daily readings. The verse is, "Your burdens shall be no more," from Isaiah 10:27. I tell him that I have been trying to memorize Bible verses and ask if he wants to memorize this one with me. He agrees, and by the end of the day, has the verse memorized.

Around that time, a new worship song from Jeremy Camp called "There Will Be a Day" starts getting played on the radio, and it is based on the verse we just memorized. It talks about the day when there will be no more tears, no more pain, and no more fears — when we see Jesus face to face. The song brings me so much peace and comfort.

A few days later, we have a family meeting with the doctors, and they tell us there is nothing more they can do.

"Your dad…what a fighter," one of the doctors says. "You can't get anything past that guy."

Shortly after the meeting, I happen to be in Dad's room alone with him.

"What did they say?" he inquires. I can see the fear in his eyes.

How do I respond? How much do I tell him?

"Well, Dad, the problem is that they don't think your heart can take any more chemo."

He looks at me with desperation in his eyes. I grab him and hug him, and sob into his shoulder.

Over the next few days, we each say our good byes in our own way.

One day as I talk with him, I feel a desire to explain how the bad relationships and problems I've had with guys over the past ten years has made me realize what a good father he has been.

"Dad, I've been with a lot of crappy guys." I begin.

He stops me and says, "You just haven't found the right one yet. You will."

"No," I quickly respond. "I didn't mean it that way. I meant to say that it's made me realize you were a great dad."

"And you've been the *best* daughter," he whispers, with a weak smile.

That Sunday, I ask my brother and my mom to watch Jamie for me so I can spend the afternoon with my father. Because I am always running after little Jamie, I haven't had as much alone time with my dad. As I sit in the room, the sound of my father's shallow, labored breaths filling the room, I begin to write a letter to my father.

"Dear Daddy, as I sit here watching you sleep, it breaks my heart to know that soon you will take your last breath and be with us no longer. As much as this hurts us, we can see what a better life you have waiting ahead of you, where your burdens shall be no more."

And that's as far as I get with my letter. My dad takes his final breath a short time later.

I'm especially thankful for the time I spent with him that beautiful Sunday, the day he left our world and entered heaven. How appropriate for Dad to go on a Sunday, because that was our favorite day. While I was growing up, after church on Sunday morning, we'd go home and I would sit on Daddy's lap as he read me the Sunday newspaper comics (we called them "the funnies"). Mom would don her apron and cook up one of her delicious Sunday dinners. We usually took a nap, and then Dad would take us on an outdoor adventure — often a long walk or an afternoon of fishing. Dad had a great appreciation for the outdoors.

My dad and brother loved to hunt. So, of course, I got dragged along on the hunting trips too. But I learned to love them and found out I was pretty good with a shotgun myself. Well, most of the time. Hunting geese with my dad one weekend, I was hunkered down in the middle of a field. My dad had used a goose call to lure a flock of geese from a far distance. As they got closer and closer, I became more anxious and excited to stand up and shoot. My dad kept yelling at me to wait. Finally, he yelled, "Get up!"

The geese were flying directly over my head. I jumped up and took my first shot, only to find out the safety was still on. By the time I got the safety off, the geese were long gone. I turned to my father, assuming he'd be frustrated and angry with me, but he had a big smile on his face and said "That's okay, you'll get em' next time!" Not my proudest moment, but a fun memory of hunting with my dad.

My father died on April 13, 2008. We put the verse he and I had memorized together on his gravestone. "Your burdens shall be no more. —Isaiah 10:27"

And, when I see a flock of geese flying overhead (which happens often), I think of my daddy, smile, and wave.

That's okay, you'll get 'em next time.

CHAPTER THIRTY-THREE
Reality Stars?

With my father gone, I have a new concern on my hands. My father and mother were always inseparable, and now my mom is alone, left to care for two homes. She still owns the home in Norcross and the farm near Aberdeen, South Dakota, where she spends a good amount of her time. I'm not concerned about her when she is in Norcross, as she has family and lifelong friends and neighbors nearby to help her out. But I am extremely nervous about the time she spends alone at the cabin.

After much soul searching, I make the difficult decision to uproot the life I had built in Rapid City over the past ten years and move to Aberdeen. When I first started in the insurance business all those years ago, I made next to nothing. Over the years, as I gained more clients and developed relationships, I built a nice business for myself. I was making really good money, working part-time, and had lots of free time to spend with my son.

I can't believe I have to leave it all behind and start over, but it is the right thing to do. It will be good to leave all the bad memories behind and get a fresh start. Besides, I am a single mom, and I really look forward to having my mom nearby to help me out.

It is hard being a single mom. Terry is not a part of Jamie's life, by his own choice. I find myself being thankful for all of the years I was a nanny. I learned so much about kids, and managing a household, and I believe the skills I learned really help me.

I buy a home without even seeing it. My mom checks it out for me. I see pictures online, make an offer, and close on it, without having ever set foot in the house. The closing date on the house is August 1, 2008, the day before my son turns two. I tell him that I bought the house for him for his birthday.

I sell my condo in Rapid City, pack up my belongings and my two year-old son, and move to Aberdeen, where I don't know a single soul.

As I am unpacking my boxes in Aberdeen, I am devastated to find out that the piano shaped music box that Kim gave me the night of my senior recital is broken. I thought I had wrapped it sufficiently, but it somehow escaped its wrapping, and the ceramic and glass are shattered into many little pieces. It is not repairable. I shed a tear as I drop it in the garbage. That music box meant so much to me.

Thankfully, Khloe's ceramic cocker spaniel survives the trip, and I place it on a shelf in my bedroom. I think about Kim, Khloe, Kourtney, and Robert, and wonder how they are doing. I have lost touch with them. The trials and tribulations of the past five years have consumed me. I still talk to Bruce every year on our birthday, and he gives me a quick update on everyone, but I haven't talked to the kids in years. I miss them, and regret that I didn't make an effort to stay connected.

I recently reconnected with Linda. I always think of her when I use the hand signals she taught me. When people compliment me, I put both hands up, one with the palm out, saying "stop," and the other waving in, as in "come on, give me more compliments." I use it often, and it always makes people laugh.

Starting over proves more difficult than I ever imagined. The insurance business is built on relationships, which take years to cultivate. The prospect of spending years to develop a new business overwhelms me, but I don't know what else to do. That's the career I know.

I find a job at a local bank as the insurance representative, but that doesn't work out so well. Sometime during the first year in Aberdeen, I sink into a deep depression. I struggle with handling the loss and change that has occurred in my life over the past few years *and* dealing with life as a single mom. I feel alone. I feel isolated. I miss my dad. I don't understand why I ended up in two disastrous relationships. I am heartbroken that my son's father isn't a part of his life.

My relationship with God suffers a bit of a setback. I have been faithful to Him for so many years with regular church attendance, Bible study, and I've certainly prayed enough to merit a few blessings. Instead, I feel like I am being punished for the bad choices I've made over the past few years. I am back to that whole guilt thing. It is an awful, heavy feeling.

What it comes down to is I don't really trust God with my love life. I haven't given that area of my life over to God. I realize I am desperate to be loved by a man. I'm not sure why. I don't know if it goes back to the date rape experience in high school. Or maybe my search for love is a result of the relationship I had with my father. I loved him so much, and I know he loved me, but I never heard those words from him. I feel like I have always yearned for acceptance. I was always grasping for approval that seemed to always elude me.

Then, I choose a husband who drinks heavily and hits me. After that, I dive into a relationship with a man who is a drug addict and serial cheater. I haven't been shown a very good image of love from the men I've been involved with.

I realize the best model I've had for how I should be treated was Bruce Jenner. He was kind of like a father figure, a big brother, and a best friend all rolled into one.

As I sort out my feelings about God, I operate on spiritual autopilot for my first couple years in Aberdeen. I check out several different churches, but don't feel comfortable at any of them. So I bounce around, not fully committing to one church for quite some time.

Eventually, I find a part-time job for another insurance company in town. That position doesn't even begin to pay the bills though, so it is time to look for a second job. I take a job as organist of a church, and find it is nice to be using my musical talents once more.

After another year of struggling financially, I decide to look for a third job. I think substitute teaching might be fun. So I apply at several local schools, and before long, get hired by the high school.

My first assignment is substitute teacher for the high school band instructor. Since I majored in music, it is perfect, and I have a blast. The kids love me, and I realize I am actually quite good at teaching. Before long, an elementary school calls me for an assignment as well. I begin to work regularly — several days per week — as a substitute teacher. The kids bring a great deal of joy into my life and help to ease the depression I had been experiencing.

It is still a constant struggle to make ends meet. I need all three jobs to pay the bills. And managing three different schedules while caring for my son alone is like juggling three balls while peddling a unicycle and balancing a clown on my head…nearly impossible.

One day, about a year after I moved to Aberdeen, I am in the grocery store check out line, and notice Kim, Kourtney, and Khloe Kardashian on the cover of a magazine. I pick it up, in shock, and read about their new reality television show, *Keeping Up with the Kardashians*. Apparently, it started airing on television the year before, but with all the craziness with my dad, having a son, working, and moving, I *never* watch TV, and I had no clue "my family" had become somewhat famous.

I still talk to Bruce every year on our birthday, but he hasn't mentioned the reality show. I lost touch with the kids over the years. I called Khloe in September 2003 when her father Robert died, and left her a message offering my condolences, but I haven't had any conversations with them since I visited them in 2000.

I buy the magazine, and as I hand it to the clerk at the checkout stand, I mention, "I used to work for them as their nanny."

She looks up at me in disbelief. "What on earth are you doing here in Aberdeen?"

For years after I left Los Angeles, whenever I told anyone that I had been the nanny for the famous Olympian Bruce Jenner, people were intrigued, and that's all they would want to talk about. I was always pegged "the former nanny to the stars." I left Los Angeles mainly because I wanted to make my *own* life, so the interest about Bruce and the "Hollywood lifestyle" really bugged me. I stopped talking about it — for years. I just wanted to be Pam.

Now that I have made my own life back in the Midwest, and the entire Kardashian family has become famous, I start talking about my nanny experience again. Everyone I speak to about it is fascinated, intrigued, and asks for stories and details about the family and what it was like working for them.

That fall, as I am talking to Bruce on our birthday, he says, "Hold on, Kris wants to talk to you."

"Oh hi sweetie pie," Kris purrs into the phone. "I wanted to talk to you about coming back to work for us."

I am so flabbergasted, I don't know what to say.

"Right now I'm looking at literally hundreds of resumes," she continues, "But if you were interested, I would throw all of them away."

We discuss the job for a few minutes, and then agree we will talk about it again in a few days. After giving the opportunity serious consideration (it is a good salary and I definitely need the money), I realize I don't want to uproot my life again and move away from my family. My mom would be devastated if I left. She is still grieving and needs me, and I need her.

Although I am struggling and could really use the money, I don't want to go back to that lifestyle. I'm glad I'm back in the Midwest. I enjoy the simple life, being around my family, and enjoying time with my son. Despite desperately needing the money, I make a choice to put my family first. But it sure is nice to know they think so highly of me, and would consider hiring me back.

I continue to struggle to make ends meet and care for my son as a single mother. One day, a friend of mine recommends a book by pastor Joel Osteen titled, *Your Best Life Now: 7 Steps to Living at Your Full Potential*. A week or so after I read it, I look in the mirror and think to myself, I miss Pam. I realize in the midst of the turmoil, heartbreak, changes, and depression I'd endured the last few years, I lost my laugh and I lost my smile. And I miss me. The me that smiles, laughs, jokes, dances, does high kicks, and has a zest for life. I make a commitment to myself at that moment, as I am looking at my reflection in the mirror. I am going to get my smile and my laugh back.

The book inspires me to make a drastic change in my life, for my sake and for my son. It takes my relationship with God to a new level. I make a choice as I am looking at my reflection in the mirror to allow God to guide every aspect of my life, including finding the right man who loves God with all his heart. I purchase a stack of white index cards, write an inspirational quote on each one, and post them up on a bulletin board in my bathroom where I can read them every day.

I watch *Keeping Up with the Kardashians* occasionally with mixed feelings. Of course, I am shocked to see the kids I took care of for so many years, all grown up, on television. I am happy for them, and for their success.

Their life seems crazy and "unreal" to many people, but having been there when they were kids, I can tell you it's their "normal." They don't know anything else. They've lived this type of lifestyle their entire lives (although not to the extreme affluence they enjoy now).

Kourtney, Kim, and Khloe are gorgeous girls, and I see that the little personalities I knew as children are still a part of them. Not a lot has changed. Kourtney is still all business. She tells it like it is — no "BS." She's smart and wise, and has a lot of common sense. Kim is more beautiful than ever. She's the fashionista, which is no surprise. She was always dressed so cute as a kid. Khloe had a feisty side to her, and I see that coming out on the show.

When I see Robert, I think back to the first time I saw him as a little four year-old boy with a bowl haircut. He is still somewhat reserved, and I see the same glint of mischievousness in his eyes.

I'd say the Kris you see on TV is exactly the Kris I knew. Business woman, mom, manager, strong, confident, at times controlling, sweet, loving, cussing up a storm one minute, and then hugging and kissing everyone with tears in her eyes the next. She wears her heart on her sleeve, and she tells it like it is.

My relationship with her was often difficult, but also sweet and loving at times. Working for her was challenging, frustrating, demanding, and ultimately, rewarding. Passionate people evoke passionate reactions, and Kris is a passionate woman. You experience the highs and the lows with Kris.

When people find out about my connection to the Kardashians, they often ask me, what was it like working for Kris? With any close relationship, there are good times and there are bad times. There are qualities you love and qualities you don't care for. And I worked *extremely* closely with Kris on a daily basis for five years, so we experienced the highs and the lows of a close relationship.

I do believe that Kris loves her family fiercely. I think she takes great pride in her role as mother. I believe her children are her most precious possessions, and that she always strives to make decisions she thinks are in her family's best interest. Back when I worked with her, I didn't always agree with her decisions, and maybe I wouldn't have made the same choices, but it was not my place to judge. My focus was on loving the children and taking the best care of them I possibly could.

At the time, I wasn't mature enough to look at it from her perspective, but now, years later, I think about how difficult it must have been to make that choice to pursue business success and put her children in the care of a nanny.

Khloe and Robert would climb on my lap and tell me they loved me, sometimes in front of Kris. That's why she paid me — to love her kids and take care of them — but I can imagine it must have bothered her sometimes. I always felt uncomfortable in those moments, worried about what she might be thinking.

Now I imagine the thoughts that might have been going through her mind, as I recall the way she would look at me when they were being affectionate with me. Was she pleased that they loved me so much and were happy in my care, or did she feel regret…or even jealousy? Did she ever question her choices? Motherhood in this age where women have incredible opportunity to pursue careers creates a difficult choice that every mother must struggle with at some point. I know I have, and there's no right answer. What's right for one mother doesn't fit another mother's lifestyle, circumstances, personality, career choices, or desires. It's a personal choice. And I respect that, so I'm not judging at all, but simply asking the question, I wonder how she felt about her choices?

I am going through some papers one day after I'd watched a few episodes of the reality show. I come across the letter of recommendation that Kris wrote to me. As I read it, tears flow down my cheeks. Again, her words of praise affect me deeply. I realize that my own profound need for acceptance and approval affected how I viewed my relationship with her.

What is it about this family? Why have they become the most successful reality show in the history of television? Why are public opinions about them so polarized? It seems that people either LOVE them or HATE them. So what is it?

I think they have the "it" factor. That indefinable, indescribable "something" that makes someone special. And we're attracted to "it." We're attracted to them. It doesn't matter whether you love them or hate them, you still want to tune in, you want to watch and listen, and know what they're up to.

Is the reality show scripted or is it real? Honestly, does it really matter? They're entertainers. I wonder…if they confirmed that it was scripted, would everyone stop watching? I doubt it, because they're interesting. They're crazy and zany. They're funny. And, it's entertaining.

I think what is so appealing to those who love them is they're normal people — a normal family with normal issues. They fight, have disagreements, suffer through disappointments, and celebrate triumphs. And despite what seems to most like a pretty crazy lifestyle — they love each other. We can identify with them.

Or, for those that hate them, could it be that they're jealous? What do they have that I don't have? Why them and not me? It's fairly easy to be happy for (or at least indifferent to) someone who is wealthy and famous because they've started a company, been a successful business executive, made a hit record, or produced or starred in a movie. But, it is more difficult to find it in your heart to be happy for people who are famous simply for being famous. They're just a normal family.

Why them? How did this "normal" family from Malibu turn out to be the famous reality stars we see on TV? I don't believe in luck, good or bad. I believe opportunities come to us, and if we're prepared, we capitalize on those opportunities. If we're not prepared, they pass us by. In my opinion, the success of the Kardashians and the empire they've built is the culmination of many years of hard work, and being prepared to capitalize on numerous opportunities when they presented themselves.

Despite all the negative press this family has received, I'd say they're a lot smarter than most give them credit for. Love them or hate them, agree with their lifestyle and choices or not, you at least have to respect the tremendous level of success they've achieved.

Although she doesn't have a college degree, Kris has an innate, keen understanding of marketing and publicity. She honed those skills while promoting Bruce and launching their business endeavors together. Those same skills helped her to launch the Kardashian brand she drives today. She is driven and focused, will not take no for an answer, and is tenacious until she has accomplished her goal. It does not surprise me at all that they have achieved their current level of stardom, wealth, and success.

I think back to my years in high school and the television and movie stars that I idolized and put on a pedestal. Unlike most people, I got to meet and interact with many of my idols. It's interesting to look at my experience and relate it to the infatuation people have today with the Kardashians. I idolized Sylvester Stallone. I was obsessed with him. I felt as though I knew him. Then I met him, and started dating him, and realized, after I got over the initial shock, that he's just a normal person.

I wonder why we idolize celebrities and spend so much time, energy, and money watching, reading, and commenting on their personal lives. Maybe it's escapism — a diversion from our own lives. Maybe we feel better about our own situations when we see celebrities making mistakes or going through drama. Or maybe it's a thirst for something different than the existence we live — more adventure and more excitement.

I know that's what I felt growing up when I idolized the stars from *Love Boat, CHiPS,* and *Charlie's Angels.* I wanted to explore and seek a thrilling life beyond my small town reality.

CHAPTER THIRTY-FOUR
California Dreamin'

In August 2011, I take a trip to California. The main reason for the trip is the fifth birthday of my son. I have been promising him forever that when he turns five, I'll take him to Disneyland. During my trip, I also plan to spend a few days with my best friend, Sara, and her family in San Diego, and with my dear friend, Smitty, and her family in Los Angeles. Also, I am excited to reunite with Linda Jenner, Brandon, and Brody. Linda and I have kept in touch, and I look forward to having the chance to see her again after almost twenty years.

We make plans to get together for lunch on a Monday. The day before, I take Jamie fishing at Troutdale, the favorite fishing spot of Brandon and Brody when they were my son's age. I think Jamie will have fun there too. We rent a couple of fishing poles, and buy pieces of corn and Velveeta cheese. As I watch Jamie fish, it takes me back twenty years when I was here with Brandon and Brody. It is a surreal moment. I think about the endless hours I spent here with the boys, and how much my life has changed in these two decades. If only I knew back then what was in store for me — the change, mistakes, loss, blessings, and miracles. I never imagined I'd be back here with my own son.

After an hour or so of fishing, Jamie is covered in dirt and grinning from ear to ear. The phone rings, and it is Linda.

"What are you doing?"

"We're at Troutdale! And Jamie's having a blast." I say.

She laughs, knowing how much time I spent there years ago with her two boys.

"I'm on my way to the Malibu house," she informs me. "Why don't you just come and see me today since you're so close?"

Troutdale is just around the corner from her house. I look at Jamie in his filthy t-shirt and shorts and cringe. I did not want glamorous Linda to meet my son for the first time when he looks like an orphan. And both my mom and I dressed to "go fishing." I look like I just came back from a workout at the gym. What the heck, I say to myself, and tell her we will be there soon.

We arrive at Linda's charming house where I spent so many years of my life. When the security gate opens to let us in, a flood of memories hit me. I feel tears welling up in my eyes and my throat tightens up as I try to keep from crying. As we drive up to the house, I imagine and hope that I will see Brandon and Brody (just the way they looked twenty years ago) running out of the house.

Linda stands by the front door waiting for us, looking like the same gorgeous beauty queen she was two decades ago. She must be about sixty now, but truly looks like she is in her forties. She is the same bubbly, joking, friendly, charming Linda that I knew and loved. It is as if time had stood still, and we pick right back up where we left off.

The house looks about the same, full of country charm, with the exception of her newest addition — an unbelievable rose garden. Row after row of breathtaking rose bushes in every variety and color fill her yard. They smell heavenly.

It is a beautiful summer day in August, so we hang out on the patio. Linda asks us if we want something to drink, and we agree. As she heads into the house, she turns around.

With a huge smile on her face, she asks, "You still dating Sly?"

We both break into hysterical laughter. Thank goodness she held no bitter feelings about the poor judgment of a young teenager.

We drink lemonade on the deck, reminiscing about the good old days, as Jamie jumps in and out of the pool. I feel an odd sense of déjà vu, because Brandon and Brody were just about Jamie's age when I took care of them, and they used to do the exact same thing.

As I watch Jamie, I realize how fleeting time is, how quickly our children grow up (it seems like only yesterday it was Brandon and Brody in that pool) and how precious these moments are with my young son. I make a promise to myself that I am not going to let these years fly by without cherishing every precious moment I have with him.

We've been chatting for a while when Linda's phone rings. It is Brandon, letting her know he is coming by the house in a few minutes.

I am so excited. I had been hoping that Brandon and Brody would join us. It has been nearly twenty years since I've seen "my boys."

Soon, a car pulls up, and out steps a tall, handsome, and all grown up Brandon. I am incredibly proud, and my heart fills with emotion. He has the same sweet smile and laid back demeanor from his youth but is about two feet taller than the last time I saw him. He is a gentleman — sweet, friendly, nice, and polite. He brings his girlfriend, Leah, along with him, and she is a beautiful, soft-spoken young lady. They are in a band together, called simply, "Brandon and Leah."

Shortly after he arrives, Brandon says to me, "Do you remember what you used to say to us every morning, to wake us up?"

"Actually, I don't. I'm sorry. Remind me." I reply, feeling bad that I don't remember something that was obviously meaningful to him.

Leah chimes in, "You don't remember? Brandon says it *every* morning, and I can even say it!"

Now I feel really bad. Even his girlfriend knows what I used to say. I can't believe I don't remember.

Brandon reminds me, "Awake! Alert, alive, and enthuuuusiastic!" he exclaims with much gusto.

As soon as he says "awake," I remember. Tears roll down my cheek. I am honored that a phrase I used twenty years ago is something he now repeats to himself every day. I hope when he has children some day he will teach the phrase to them too.

I am sad that I don't get to see Brody, but he is on his way to Las Vegas for his 28th birthday party.

It is a very special and wonderful reunion, and so good to see two people that I loved dearly, who were such a huge part of my life for so many years.

When we get home from our trip, I decide to start waking my own son the same way. He loves it…just about as much as Brandon and Brody did. Give him twenty years, though, and my hope is he'll be repeating it to himself every morning, just like Brandon.

A few days later, after my return to Aberdeen, a co-worker at my insurance office asks, "When did life get so crazy? Do you remember the last time you were carefree and happy go lucky?"

I don't have to think about it too long. It was the first two years that I was a nanny. We spent our days in the California sunshine, laughing, playing, and being young (I was really still a kid myself) and carefree. I loved those two boys so much. I gave them advice, I disciplined them, I protected them as best I could, but most of all…I loved them.

I think about "Grown Up Christmas List," which has become a popular Christmas classic. Every time I hear it, I remember Linda, David and the boys, and that magical vacation in British Columbia. I have so many great memories of those two years with Linda, Brandon and Brody.

Reuniting with Brandon and Linda after all of these years meant so much to me. Hearing Brandon share his memories of me, touched me deeply. I realize anew that being a nanny was a wonderful gift and blessing. What an honor to be such an integral part of shaping the lives of those young children.

CHAPTER THIRTY-FIVE
Living the Adventure

It is a surprising coincidence that my trip to California happens to fall on the same weekend as Kim's wedding to Kris Humphries. I had hoped to reunite with Bruce and Kris and some of the Kardashian kids as well, but everyone is in Santa Barbara for the wedding.

A few months later, the marriage is over. I feel bad that Kim receives such a negative reaction about her seventy-two day marriage to Kris. Many people think it is a hoax — a stunt to make money and garner publicity.

As Kim is going through the aftermath of her divorce, I speak to Bruce on the phone one day, and all he can talk about is how he and Kris and the entire family are so upset that Kim is receiving such backlash from the public about the marriage. If they had orchestrated that entire event, I think they'd be happy about the publicity, good or bad, knowing upfront there would be immense negative publicity for such a blatant scheme.

My opinion is Kim really fell in love with him. I think she got carried away with the "idea" of love. She had just turned thirty, which I know is a significant marker for many women, a target many of us have set for marriage and children. It certainly was for me, and probably the reason I married Ryan. Was Kim measuring herself against her sisters? Khloe is happily married. Kourtney has been with Scott for years, has a young son, and a daughter on the way.

Just like she did when she was a child, I believe Kim yearned for true love and a family of her own so deeply she willed it to happen. And, she got swept up in the storybook romance. When there were signs Kris was likely not the best match for her, she might have overlooked them, because she wanted the "happily ever after" so badly, or maybe because it was too far along in the planning of the extravagant affair and she couldn't turn back. Could it be she didn't want to disappoint everyone, or did she brush off her misgivings as nervous wedding jitters? Regardless of the reasons, I believe it boils down to her strong, lifelong desire to be a wife and a mom.

And I can relate. There were many red flags with Ryan, and in retrospect, I knew in my heart it wouldn't last, but I wanted marriage and babies so badly, I moved forward with blinders on.

I hear many people questioning why she didn't stay in the marriage longer and try to work it out. To me, that just proves she already had reservations going in, and they were quickly confirmed once she was married and living together. Anyone who has been married or lived together realizes you don't *really* know someone until you live together.

I think about my wedding night, as I was lying on the bed next to my passed-out husband, knowing in my heart I had made a mistake. I wonder if she knew on her wedding day she was making a mistake? I can relate so much to what she has been through, and I wish we hadn't lost contact, and I was there to support her through that.

A few months later, in January of 2012, I am appalled and heartbroken to hear the revelations from Robert Kardashian's widow, Ellen that Khloe is not Robert's daughter. My personal opinion is Robert *was* Khloe's biological father. But regardless of paternity, what is a father? A father is the man who raises you, supports you, encourages you, instills morals and values, spends time with you, and loves you unconditionally. And that is exactly what Robert did for Khloe. I was an eyewitness to the very special bond they shared. They loved each other dearly.

Khloe and the other kids were fortunate because they had two fathers — Robert *and* Bruce. When Bruce and Kris got married, Bruce willingly and whole-heartedly assumed the role of stepfather. He was loving, encouraging, and patient with all the kids. No matter what the scandalous claims may be, Khloe is blessed to have two dads that loved her very much.

Not long after, I am surprised and thrilled to find out that Bruce is going to be in Aberdeen, SD. The local boys and girls club is planning a big gala dinner to raise funds for the construction of a new building, and they choose Bruce as their keynote speaker. No celebrities *ever* come to Aberdeen. I chalk it up to serendipity once again.

The committee chairman and his wife happen to be friends of mine, so we plan for me to go with them to the airport to pick Bruce up. In mid-February, on a Friday night, I arrived in the small (only one gate) airport in Aberdeen to await Bruce's arrival.

When he sees me, his face breaks into a wide grin. "You're here too?" he exclaims.

We agree to talk the next morning and end up meeting for lunch on Saturday. I bring my mom and Jamie along. Bruce has never met my son. We have a great time, reconnecting after all of these years. Bruce is wonderful with Jamie, teasing him and talking to him during lunch. It reminds me of Brandon and Brody, and the many times we sat around a table laughing and joking, but now it is my own son.

Saturday evening at the dinner event, I get a chance to hear Bruce's inspirational speech for the first time. In all the years I worked for them, I never heard Bruce speak publicly.

He describes how he got started in track and field, and then decides to pursue a dream of making it to the Olympics. He shares that the turning point for him was when he asked himself, what is the single most important thing in my life? When he realized the answer was winning a gold medal at the Olympics, it changed everything. Every moment of his entire life became dedicated to achieving that goal.

After practicing all day, he'd go home to his apartment at night where there was a hurdle set up in his living room, and he'd practice his form for hours more. At night, he'd dream about running and winning the medal. It became his obsession and led to his world record time in winning the Gold Medal in the decathlon in the 1976 Olympics.

Bruce has a gift. He is incredibly inspirational. Listening to him reminds me of our trips to Tahoe, and the sports he tried to teach me, like skiing and golf. He never let me say "I can't" or "I won't." I always had to try my best and keep at it. He truly understands the power of positive thinking. I learned so many things from Bruce. He often told me "if you have a goal you want to accomplish, make a decision in your mind that you will let *nothing* dissuade you from it." He believed that attitude and the mind are very powerful. He always told me, "never give up, never say no, always believe in yourself, and always stay positive." Those inspirational messages have stuck with me through the years.

Now that Bruce has seen my life, and met my son, I feel like everything has come full circle. Watching him with Jamie and remembering the years I spent with Brandon and Brody make me realize how every little step in my journey was preparing me for this moment — my role as a mother. This is my grandest adventure and my greatest achievement. If any of the steps along the way hadn't happened, I might not have Jamie.

When I reflect on my experience in Los Angeles and how it affected me, I realize it was eye opening for me, and it helped me clarify what I do and don't want in life. I don't ever want money to change my morals, beliefs, or values. And, I really do want a simple, quiet life with a good man, a close family, and dear friends.

I think back to those years in Hollywood and how immature and naïve I was. Drinking and driving, and keeping my relationship with Sly a secret from Linda were mistakes and lapses in judgment, but I learned and grew from each and every experience.

I reflect on some of my poor choices in men, and the years of heartache it caused. Yet, even the *worst* mistake of all — my choice to stand by Terry — was an integral part of the plan. I spent years in depression, much of it a result of the loss and the indescribable, deep pain of betrayal from that relationship. I couldn't understand. I was dedicated, loyal, and gave up my life for him. But, God specializes in redeeming bad choices. Now I look at all that pain, and where I am now, and I say *this* is why! Every bit of that horrible pain was worth it to have this most precious gift. My son Jamie is my miracle — my blessing from God.

I've learned through my son, and as I've grown closer to God, what selfless love is. I recognize that my vision of love was skewed because of my experiences with men. I wonder, if Jamie wasn't in my life, would I have followed the same pattern, going from man to man, trying to fill the holes in my soul with a person, instead of with God.

It's been six years since I kicked Terry out of my house after being lied to and betrayed. I've dated a few guys here and there, but have yet to find the love of my life. I am waiting on God's "Plan A" for my life. I know he has a man out there made specifically for me. A man that loves God first and foremost, but someone who will also love me and my son the way we deserve to be loved. I want to be deeply and passionately in love. I know it will happen. I'm just leaving it up to God and opening my heart to the possibility, so I can see him when he steps into my life.

We have free will, and we get to make our own choices in this life. When things go smoothly, it's easy to lose perspective about what's important. I think that's why God allows heartache and challenges in our lives, because it's only when times are tough that we feel unsettled, look around, begin to question things, and ask, "Is there more to life than this?"

I'm not perfect, and I never will be. It's not like I've finally arrived, or I suddenly have all the answers. I continue to make mistakes, poor choices, and bad decisions all the time. But that's where grace comes in. I've realized God offers complete grace and love, and I've learned to offer the same to myself. I can be graceful with my soul when I've messed up. It's not about living up to the rules or striving to be a "good girl." God loves me regardless of what I do. But when I am in a right relationship with him, I *desire* to make decisions and choices that feel right with my soul — that keep my heart and soul in balance and harmony with God.

I've given up the God of "religion" that I grew up with, along with the list of rules, guilt, and failure. I've come to know a God that is so much more than that. My God accepts me, mistakes, blemishes, and all. He already knows the real me, and I don't need to pretend or "clean up my act" before I approach Him. He wants me to be real with Him, just as I am, right in that moment. He invites me to bare myself to Him whether I am screaming, crying, or laughing. He always listens and always loves me. No matter what mistakes I have made, no matter how badly I have messed up, I can go to Him and He will accept me, love me, and forgive me.

I am reminded of God's grace and love every time I hear the song, "Amazing Grace." I often sit down at the piano and play it. The melody speaks to my heart of the loving and gracious God I have come to know.

My favorite Bible verse from Proverbs talks about how God will take care of me, as long as I trust in Him, even when I'm not sure exactly what's going on. Proverbs 3: 5-7 says, "*Trust in the LORD with all your heart; and lean not on your own understanding. In all your ways acknowledge him, and he shall direct your paths.*" I've learned that's really how God works. Often in the midst of difficulties, it's impossible to see a way out of the situation, but God knows and He can help me, as long as I will allow Him to guide me. Looking back, I see how God has had His hand on me every step of the way.

My journey through life has been a wild ride, full of twists, turns, and crazy adventures — from my years in Hollywood to the hills of Tennessee, through broken relationships, to the birth of my precious son and the death of my beloved father. When I look back over my life, I realize I've been guided by a set of principles. I've found when I follow these "rules" — although my life isn't perfect and things don't always turn out how I hope or expect — I am living authentically and adventurously.

Nanny Pam's Guide to Living Adventurously

1) Connect with God. Honestly, I can't imagine waking up each and every day and facing the challenges this life holds without the knowledge that there is something more. Believing in God and knowing that He is holding me in the palm of His hand, despite the circumstances, gives me hope.

Through the darkly shaded glasses of my childhood religious experience, the God who loves me and defies any stereotypes and definitions somehow emerged. As the reality of life hit me in my late thirties — failures, deep hurts, disappointments, searing losses, blessings and miracles — I transitioned to a real, intimate relationship with God. And, over the last few years, I've become completely and utterly reliant on Him. Life can be really hard sometimes. I can't imagine suffering through the tragedies and difficult seasons I've experienced without God, or without the knowledge that there's something bigger and better for all of us than this life we're living now. Knowing God and believing in Heaven places my focus on the important things — family, friends, relationships, loving and helping people, caring about one another, and making the right decisions when it really counts.

I've also found when I'm seeking God, talking to Him and asking Him to guide me, amazingly enough, He answers. It's when I'm not reaching for Him, and not listening to my heart (and His), that I get into trouble. Through this real and honest, give and take relationship with God, I've found peace and happiness I've never before experienced.

I believe our spirits desire to connect with their creator. We have a hole in our heart that can only be filled with God. So I strive to always be moving *towards* God, however that looks. And it's a constantly evolving process. I'm not always consistent. We go through ups and downs, God and me. But it's a real relationship that needs tending, and so it is a priority in my daily life.

2) Follow your heart. For me, this is a critical way to live. Yes, sometimes it has gotten me into trouble. Yet, I will always believe that following my heart is the best policy. It means doing what feels authentically right to my soul. Listening to my spirit — the essence of who I am. God has instilled unique and deep desires and dreams in each of our hearts. And we must follow that or risk living a life that is a shadow of what it could be. Don't settle for less. What are your dreams? What does your heart desire? Listen to the inner voice that seeks to guide you.

3) Be true to yourself. Each of us knows in our heart the values and ideals for our life that we hold sacred. Do we allow that to guide us or are we easily influenced by others? Stay true to your values. Don't allow other people or circumstances to lead you into something that doesn't feel good to your soul. At the end of the day, each of us needs to be able to look in the mirror and say, I'm proud of the person I was today. I'm proud of the things I did, the words I said, the choices I made, and the way I treated others. Don't compromise your ideals or values…EVER.

4) Be positive — always! Anyone who knows me knows I am crazy and zany. I crack jokes constantly and have no problem looking silly or goofy to break the tension or make someone laugh. I am happy go lucky, fun loving, and love to laugh. I believe we hold an incredible power in the palm of our hand — the CHOICE about how we view the world. In my world, the glass is ALWAYS half full. It truly is a choice. You can color your world with bright colors or with shades of gray. We can change a situation simply by how we choose to view it. Interject some positivity into any situation and see what happens.

5) Always believe in the best in others. This rule has gotten me into trouble more than once, especially with men. But that doesn't change my philosophy. If I go into any situation, a new encounter, or a relationship with walls up and fear in my heart, then I am not open to receive the full benefit of that experience. I've put boundaries on it.

I truly believe that in most cases, human beings live up to the expectations you set for them. If you expect a child to misbehave and treat them accordingly, they will give you exactly what you expected. The same is true for adults. I don't want to be the reason that anyone's potential is limited, so I always choose to believe the best about others.

Sometimes I'm disappointed and hurt, but more often than not, I'm delighted and surprised by how people meet and exceed my expectations. Set the bar low and people will give you just what you expect — disappointment. But, set the bar high — and most people will live up to it.

6) Go for it! Take a chance. Risk everything. Take a step of faith. Yes, you might fall flat on your face. Reaching your dreams might take longer than you ever expected, and you might not attain the outcome you expected. But, you just might have the adventure of your life in the process. An adventure you would have missed if you hadn't risked everything and stepped out in faith. Sometimes, amazing things happen just because you put yourself out there. You meet new people, have new experiences, expand your horizons, and find yourself in a life changing moment that wouldn't have occurred if you hadn't opened your heart to new possibilities.

There's nothing worse than a dream never pursued. Notice I didn't say "dream never fulfilled." Big difference. Many times our dreams don't end up being fulfilled exactly how we expected. But what is most important is that you take the step toward that dream. At least you can always say, I tried. I gave it my best shot. I can't imagine anything worse than looking back at the end of my life with a long list of dreams that I never pursued and having horrible regrets that I never even tried. I may fail. I may not achieve exactly what I set out to do, but at least I tried. From my experience, an amazing thing happens when you step out in faith. You discover new dreams, or the original dream shifts or changes focus.

7) Do not let fear stop you! This principal is incredibly important, powerful, and life changing. Many people live their life in fear. Fear of the unknown, fear of the future, of disappointment, of hurt, of what might happen, of opening their heart, of taking risks. The list goes on and on. I'm sure anyone reading this could insert his or her own list. What is your greatest fear?

Fear is a wasted emotion. It prevents us from moving forward or taking action. Fear paralyzes. What I've realized is that fear hyper-focuses our minds on ONE possible outcome, ignoring the many other possible positive outcomes. It is a mindset that restricts and limits your potential. I CHOOSE to be open and push past fear and open my heart to living adventurously.

I'm thankful for every experience I've had, even the hard ones. I'm grateful for the lessons I've learned as a result and the wisdom I've gained along the way. My decade in Hollywood was the setting for many fun memories, and I'm thankful for how those events shaped me and lead me full circle to this sacred space in my life.

My deepest hope and desire is that my story has somehow inspired you to pursue a new dream, take a risk, laugh out loud more often, or do a high kick "just because." Life truly is an adventure, full of twists and turns and exciting opportunities. I hope that you will make the choice to live YOUR life adventurously!

ACKNOWLEDGEMENTS

First and foremost, I want to say thank you to my dear sweet son, Jamie. You are the love of my life! Your smile lights up each and every day, and I'm thankful that I've been given the blessing of being your mother.

Secondly, thank you to Brandon, Brody, Burt, Casey, Kourtney, Kim, Khloe, and Robert. I have so many happy memories of the years I spent with you. I loved each of you so much and took care of you as if you were my own. I'm honored that I got to be a part of your life. I am proud of each of you and think of you often. I hope you always remember your crazy Nanny Pam.

Thanks to my mom for all the years of love, encouragement and help, and for your belief in and assistance with this book.

Thank you to my life long best friend, and now author, Sara Christenson. Saree, you have done an absolutely amazing job as my voice. No one could have written my story better. Thank you from the bottom of my heart for all of your hard work. I love you dearly!

Thank you to my pastor for your wise counsel and belief in my intentions, and for the feedback on the manuscript. Thanks also to Donna, Josh, and Caitlin for reviewing the manuscript. Thank you to each and every child I taught at Aberdeen Christian School and the Roncalli Schools. You have no idea how much your support, prayers, and constant enthusiasm about this book impacted me, and I love each one of you.

Sara and I would like to give special thanks to our partners, Kristi Day and Eldon & Jannine Swingler, for their support of this book. We couldn't have done it without you. Thanks to our awesome editor, Jennifer Pooley, for her superb job of editing. Thanks also to Sabrina, Jonathan, and Janet for all of your hard work on this project.

Finally, both Sara and I want to say THANK YOU to all of our dear friends and family who believed in us and cheered us on throughout the process of writing this book. We love you!   — PJB

A Portion of our Book Sales Goes to Charity

Save the Children

When disaster strikes around the world, Save the Children is there to save lives with food, medical care and education and remains to help communities rebuild through long-term recovery programs. As quickly and as effectively as Save the Children responds to tsunamis and civil conflict, it works to resolve the ongoing struggles children face every day — poverty, hunger, illiteracy and disease — and replaces them with hope for the future.

Learn more at www.savethechildren.org